DATE DUE

Affectionately Yours

Affectionately Yours

The Letters of
Sir John A. Macdonald
and His Family

Edited and with an introduction by
J. K. Johnson

Toronto / Macmillan of Canada / 1969

Printed in Canada
by The Hunter Rose Company for
The Macmillan Company of Canada Limited,
70 Bond Street, Toronto

PREFACE

This is not a "selection" from the Macdonald family's letters but a residue. The letters that appear in this book are all that remains of a correspondence which, it is clear, was originally much more extensive. In the present collection there are many long and puzzling chronological gaps. They are gaps which, regrettably, cannot now be filled.

The letters in this book have been assembled from three sources. One letter, number 181, is the property of Macdonald Public School, Kingston, Ontario. The following letters are from the Queen's University Archives, Queen's University, Kingston: numbers 39, 46, 55, 64, 67, 80, 84, 86, 87, 91, 95, 99, 100, 102, 105, 109, 110, 114, 117, 118, 127, 130, 132, 134, 135, 138, 139, 141, 142, 144, 145, 147, 148, 149, 151, 153, 156, 161, 170, 172, 178, 179, 180, 182, 183, 184, 185, 186, 188, 189, 190, 191, 192, 194, 200, 201, 202, 203, 204, and 205. All of the other letters printed here are in the Macdonald Papers at the Public Archives of Canada, Ottawa. Permission to reproduce these letters has very kindly been granted by Mrs. Maureen Clench, Principal of Macdonald Public School, Mr. John H. Archer, Archivist of Queen's University, and Dr. W. Kaye Lamb, Dominion Archivist.

The photograph of the study at Bellevue House is reproduced by permission of the National Film Board. For permission to use all the other photographs thanks are due to the Public Archives of Canada.

J.K.J.

December 1968

CONTENTS

Affectionately Yours

INTRODUCTION

It is not surprising that the central figure of this book, and the author or recipient of the majority of the letters, is Sir John A. Macdonald himself. So far as the Macdonald family was concerned, this central role is entirely appropriate, for during the time in which these letters were written he was not only the most publicly prominent member of the family but also its actual head and principal breadwinner, his father having died in 1841. The family's correspondence revolves around him. Of course the letters of the famous are more likely to survive than those of lesser beings, but this fact alone does not explain the preponderance of his letters among the family correspondence. To an increasing degree, all his adult life, he was the counsellor, guardian, and final arbiter of the Macdonald clan in Canada.

This book contains 205 letters. Although only two of them were written before Macdonald's political career began, it is by no means a political book. There are, in fact, surprisingly few references to his public life. When he sought political advice it was not from members of his family, and they, in turn, did not (very often) attempt to influence their famous kinsman. But, if he did not need their advice, it is plain that he needed their affection and their approval. He was not always a faithful political correspondent, but throughout his life he wrote frequent and regular family letters, which sometimes reported his progress in the world and his triumphs, great and small. His letters to his mother and his sisters, especially, contain a persistent strain of boyish boastfulness. In at least one way the young man of 1842, recounting for his mother the names of the great and the near great he had seen on his first trip to England, and the statesman of 1888, sending on a letter from Lord Lansdowne to his sister "to show you the terms Lord L. and I were on", are very much the same. To his mother and his sisters he could boast a little, without fear of ridicule.

Macdonald did not use his family merely to indulge a juvenile egoism. He was, by turn, a dutiful son, a fond husband and father, a protective brother, and an indulgent grandfather. He was genuinely fond of all his near relations and, since he ordinarily saw most of them only seldom, he liked to hear news of home. It was he who kept in touch, even when they were less faithful correspondents. Often enough it was Macdonald, the over-busy politician, who reminded others of their obligations. The family was a source of solace and stability for Macdonald and he in turn was the object of a quiet, but very great, pride. From a time in early life he was an important man who, before the admiring eyes of his family, became a great man. It is small wonder that the family quickly took his leadership for granted.

The letters that John A. Macdonald wrote to his family are not exactly "great man" letters, but, even as routine correspondence, they have a certain distinction. He is easily the best letter-writer of the people represented in this book. Even the kind of non-letters which he mostly wrote during his years as prime minister – two or three sentences written in a large hand over a whole page – often sparkle with wit and dash. The letters that he received from his family have their own fascination. They are often informative, good-natured, sometimes amusing, but they lack flair. John A. Macdonald, in this as in many other ways, stood a notch above his contemporaries.

Because John A. Macdonald is probably the best-known Canadian in our history, he, of all the members of his family, needs the least advance explanation. His career, which may be studied at length in a wide range of sources, most notably in the graceful and persuasive two-volume biography by Professor Donald Creighton, will here be summarized only briefly. He was born in Glasgow in 1815,[1] to Hugh Macdonald, merchant, and his wife, the former Helen Shaw. In 1820 Hugh Macdonald brought his family to Kingston, Upper Canada. There young John Alexander

---

[1]There is, curiously, some doubt about the actual date. The official record of his birth on file at the General Register Office, Edinburgh, gives his date of birth as January 10, but it may possibly have been so recorded in error. At any rate Sir John's father entered his son's date of birth in his memorandum book (of 1820) as January 11. If the record at the Register Office is correct, a great many people, including Macdonald himself in his lifetime, have been celebrating his birthday on the wrong day for over a hundred and fifty years.

Macdonald attended school and at the age of fifteen began the study of law in the office of a Scottish lawyer, George Mackenzie. In 1836, at the age of twenty-one, he opened his first law office and began his professional career. He entered public life early, first as an alderman of Kingston, and in 1844 as Kingston's member of the Legislative Assembly of the United Province of Canada. Three years later he was taken into the provincial ministry, and he served in 1847-8, first as Receiver General and then as Commissioner of Crown Lands. After a period in opposition he returned to office in 1854 as Attorney General, Canada West. On November 27, 1857, he became, at the age of forty-two, Premier of the Province of Canada. He was an eleventh-hour convert to the idea of a federation of British North America in 1864, but, once converted, he provided most of the political management which made that idea a reality. As every Canadian schoolboy knows, he was chosen first prime minister of the new Dominion of Canada in 1867, a position he held, except for an interval of five years, until his death in 1891. During the latter years of his life, Macdonald, more than any other Canadian, imposed a degree of nation-hood on a stubbornly disparate and ridiculously attenuated collection of former colonies and territories. By the time of his death on June 6, 1891, he had become a kind of Canadian institution, the most durable of all Canadian legends.

There are twelve principal characters in this book – John A. Macdonald and eleven others, all closely connected by birth or marriage. The letters they wrote to or about one another are highly self-revealing. They do not, however, always make clear everything that one would like to know, even about the family itself. Because all of these people with the exception of Sir John A. Macdonald, and the possible exception of his son Sir Hugh, are all now more or less obscure, they require introduction in some detail, or at least in such detail as can now be assembled.

The basic family network, the Shaw-Clark-Macpherson-Macdonald connection, was complex. Since John A. Macdonald and his first wife, Isabella Clark, were cousins, the most convenient starting-point in the family history is where their two families converge. This convergence is embodied in the person of John A. Macdonald's, and Isabella Clark's, maternal grandmother, Margaret Shaw.

Margaret Shaw was born Margaret Grant, and she was twice married. Both of her husbands were named Shaw. As a result she had two families, both of which bore the same family name. By her first husband, William Shaw, she had two daughters, Margaret and Anna. By her second marriage to James Shaw, who was not related to her first husband, she had three boys, James, William, and Alexander, and one girl, Helen. Out of these two Shaw families arose three separate additional complications in the next generation. Both Anna Shaw and her sister Margaret married army officers, named, respectively, Donald Macpherson and Alexander Clark. Both sisters had large families, and eventually one of Anna's nine children, John Alexander Macpherson, married his cousin Maria, one of the ten children of Margaret Clark. Helen Shaw, the only daughter in Margaret's second family, became the mother of John A. Macdonald, and her half-sister, Margaret, was the mother of Isabella Clark, Macdonald's first wife. Macdonald and Isabella were therefore half first cousins. A third totally improbable transatlantic interconnection was established via a prominent American family, the Greenes. James Shaw, Helen Shaw's brother, emigrated to the United States and married Louisa Catherine Greene, daughter of General Nathanael Greene of Rhode Island and Georgia. James Shaw's step-niece, Margaret Clark (sister of Isabella and Maria Clark), also went to America and later married John Ward Greene, the general's nephew and a first cousin of Louisa Catherine Greene.[2] It is this Margaret Greene whose letter to John A. Macdonald begins the collected correspondence of the Macdonald family and to whom most of the earliest letters by Macdonald are addressed.

Margaret Clark, afterwards Margaret Greene, was born at Dalnavert, Inverness-shire, in 1798, and was thus seventeen years older than John A. Macdonald. It is not possible to be certain about when or why she came to America, but a number of circumstances allow a fairly enlightened guess. Her original contact must have been James Shaw, who, though he lived in Georgia, kept in close touch with his Highland relatives and who seems to have been particularly attached to his half-sister Margaret and her daughter. At any rate, they both received special bequests in his will – the mother was given property and the younger Margaret received two thousand dollars.[3] Margaret, the daughter, may perhaps have accompanied James Shaw on a return trip to Georgia, possibly when her father, Alexander Clark, died in 1819. If she did first cross the Atlantic at that time, her visit with her uncle was brief, for James Shaw also died, early in 1820. Margaret, thus twice orphaned, found a protector in John Ward

[2]He was also her second cousin on her mother's side, but that is another story.
[3]Georgia, Department of Archives and History, Atlanta, Georgia. Camden County, Wills Book "A", Will of James Shaw of Camden County, May 7, 1819.

Greene, to whom she was married in May 1822. In August of the same year John Ward Greene, too, died suddenly. Margaret Greene was once more alone, a widow at the age of twenty-four.

The family of which Margaret Greene's brief marriage had made her a part was no ordinary American family. Since 1635 when John Greene, surgeon of Salisbury, had come from England to America, the Greenes of Rhode Island had prospered greatly and had conscientiously served their colony and their state. They had become Rhode Island merchants, ship-owners, and, most importantly, foundry owners. Their family history included a colonial governor and a state governor as well as their most famous son, Major-General Nathanael Greene, who served during the Revolutionary War in several capacities with great distinction, ultimately as commander of the American Southern Army.

John Ward Greene's maternal ancestors, the Wards, were no less distinguished. Both his grandfather and his great-grandfather Ward had also been governors of Rhode Island. The Wards, among other things, claimed an unbroken record of service from 1714 to 1797, during which time some member of the family was continuously either Secretary of State or Governor of Rhode Island.

It is reasonable to ask how the Scottish Clarks and Shaws, a proud but impecunious race of Highland soldiers, came to intermarry with such a distant, powerful, and foreign dynasty. Obviously, Margaret Greene's entry into the family was a sort of sequel to the previous marriage of her uncle to the famous general's daughter, but how and when did James Shaw meet and marry Louisa Catherine Greene? On this point even speculation is of small avail. Was James Shaw a soldier? Did he fight in the Revolutionary War, and if so on which side? There are apparently no answers to these questions. All that can be said is that the transplantation of James Shaw from his native Inverness-shire glen to Camden County, Georgia, if inexplicable, is not really surprising. The Shaws were all nomadic, adventuresome, and short-lived. Before James Shaw died in 1820, one of his brothers had been killed in a duel and the other brother had died far from home.[4] The girl, Helen, the mother of John A. Macdonald, also left home, first for Glasgow, and eventually for the wilds of British North America. They had pride and ambition and a certain

---

[4]Louisa Macdonald to Macdonald, March 28, 1879. The assumption that both William and Alexander Shaw predeceased James is based on the fact that they alone, of his brothers and sisters, are not mentioned in his will.

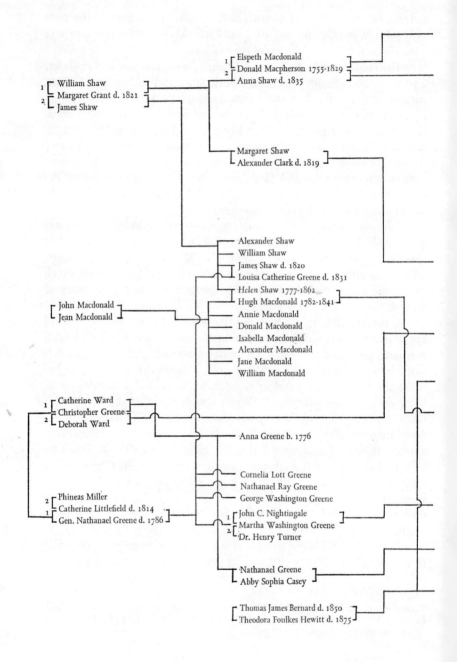

1 ⌜ William Shaw
2 ⌊ Margaret Grant d. 1821
  ⌊ James Shaw

1 ⌜ Elspeth Macdonald
2 ⌊ Donald Macpherson 1755-1829
  ⌊ Anna Shaw d. 1835

⌜ Margaret Shaw
⌊ Alexander Clark d. 1819

⌜ John Macdonald
⌊ Jean Macdonald

⌜ Alexander Shaw
⌊ William Shaw
⌊ James Shaw d. 1820
  Louisa Catherine Greene d. 1831
  Helen Shaw 1777-1862
  Hugh Macdonald 1782-1841
  Annie Macdonald
  Donald Macdonald
  Isabella Macdonald
  Alexander Macdonald
  Jane Macdonald
  William Macdonald

1 ⌜ Catherine Ward
  ⌊ Christopher Greene
2 ⌊ Deborah Ward

⌜ Anna Greene b. 1776

  Cornelia Lott Greene
  Nathanael Ray Greene
  George Washington Greene

2 ⌜ Phineas Miller
  ⌊ Catherine Littlefield d. 1814
1 ⌊ Gen. Nathanael Greene d. 1786

1 ⌜ John C. Nightingale
  ⌊ Martha Washington Greene
2 ⌊ Dr. Henry Turner

⌜ Nathanael Greene
⌊ Abby Sophia Casey

⌜ Thomas James Bernard d. 1850
⌊ Theodora Foulkes Hewitt d. 1875

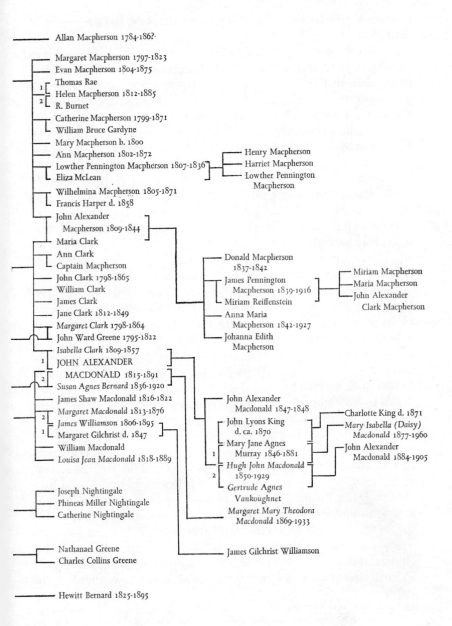

Allan Macpherson 1784-186?·

Margaret Macpherson 1797-1823
Evan Macpherson 1804-1875
Thomas Rae
1 Helen Macpherson 1812-1885
2 R. Burnet
Catherine Macpherson 1799-1871
William Bruce Gardyne
Mary Macpherson b. 1800
Ann Macpherson 1802-1872
Lowther Pennington Macpherson 1807-1836
Eliza McLean
    Henry Macpherson
    Harriet Macpherson
    Lowther Pennington
        Macpherson
Wilhelmina Macpherson 1805-1871
Francis Harper d. 1858
John Alexander
    Macpherson 1809-1844
Maria Clark
Ann Clark
Captain Macpherson
John Clark 1798-1865
William Clark
James Clark
Jane Clark 1812-1849
Margaret Clark 1798-1864
John Ward Greene 1795-1822
Isabella Clark 1809-1857
1 JOHN ALEXANDER
    MACDONALD 1815-1891
2 Susan Agnes Bernard 1836-1920
James Shaw Macdonald 1816-1822
2 Margaret Macdonald 1813-1876
    James Williamson 1806-1895
1 Margaret Gilchrist d. 1847
William Macdonald
Louisa Jean Macdonald 1818-1889

Donald Macpherson
    1837-1842
James Pennington
    Macpherson 1839-1916
Miriam Reiffenstein
Anna Maria
    Macpherson 1842-1927
Johanna Edith
    Macpherson

Miriam Macpherson
Maria Macpherson
John Alexander
    Clark Macpherson

John Alexander
    Macdonald 1847-1848
John Lyons King
    d. ca. 1870
1 Mary Jane Agnes
    Murray 1846-1881
2 Hugh John Macdonald
    1850-1929
Gertrude Agnes
    Vankoughnet
Margaret Mary Theodora
    Macdonald 1869-1933

Charlotte King d. 1871
Mary Isabella (Daisy)
    Macdonald 1877-1960
John Alexander
    Macdonald 1884-1905

Joseph Nightingale
Phineas Miller Nightingale
Catherine Nightingale

Nathanael Greene
Charles Collins Greene

James Gilchrist Williamson

Hewitt Bernard 1825-1895

restlessness which could take them far from the place, and the station, of their birth.

After the death of her husband in 1822, Margaret Greene disappears from view, to re-emerge twenty years later, near Douglas, Isle of Man. It is evident that much of the intervening period was spent in a number of cities in the United States; she could not otherwise have acquired the widespread circle of American acquaintances who come and go in her letters of the 1840s. Almost certainly she had also been to Kingston, Upper Canada, to visit her sister, Maria Macpherson, and had met her numerous aunts, uncles, and cousins there, among them young John Alexander Macdonald. At some time during those years, presumably on the death of her mother, she had taken charge of her two younger, unmarried sisters, Isabella and Jane. There is a certain amount of internal evidence in the Macdonald-Greene letters to suggest that at times all three sisters may have lived in the United States, as well as in Great Britain. At any rate, early in 1842 they were in residence in a Manx farmhouse eagerly anticipating a visit from their Canadian cousin.

No discernible family connection took them to the Isle of Man. More likely a temporary need for economy in Margaret Greene's financial affairs accounts for their being there, for living costs on the island were notoriously low and Douglas was a well-known haven for decayed gentlefolk eking out small pensions or avoiding mainland creditors. The three sisters did not, however, stay long at the island farmhouse. A turn in fortune took Margaret Greene back to Georgia in 1843, for by a deed drawn in November of that year she came into possession of the Greene family's ancestral estate.[5]

After the Revolutionary War, the grateful citizens of Georgia had presented General Nathanael Greene with Mulberry Grove Plantation, near Savannah. The general, who had spent most of his personal fortune on his army, gladly accepted the gift and before long became a Southern planter. Before his death in 1786, he added to his Georgia holdings by buying a number of small parcels of land on Cumberland Island, well to the south of Savannah, near the Florida coast. When the General's widow remarried in 1796, she and her new husband, the Honourable Phineas Miller, a state senator and Inferior Court justice, began to build an immense mansion on Cumberland Island. When it was finished, the

[5]Georgia Archives. Camden County, Book "O", page 133. Deed from Martha W. Turner to Mrs. Margaret Greene, widow, drawn November 9, 1843, recorded April 2, 1846.

8

new house, "Dungeness", with its surrounding acres of gardens and terraces, was unsurpassed in grandeur and elegance along the entire Georgia coast. Its many rooms became a home or a gathering-place for several generations of Greenes, Millers, Nightingales, and Shaws, and the centre, for a time, of a glittering social life.[6]

Nathanael Greene's widow, Catherine Littlefield Greene Miller, left Dungeness to her youngest daughter, Louisa Catherine Greene Shaw, wife of the elusive James Shaw, Margaret Greene's (and John A. Macdonald's) uncle.[7] When Louisa Shaw died in 1831, the family fortunes had substantially declined. Dungeness was sold to satisfy the debts of her estate. It was bought in August 1843 by another of the general's daughters, Martha Washington Greene Nightingale Turner,[8] re-sold in the same year to Margaret Greene, who in turn entered into an agreement with Martha Turner's son (by her first marriage), Phineas M. Nightingale, by which Nightingale acquired the use of the plantation, and Margaret Greene received an income for the next ten years,[9] before selling Dungeness to Nightingale outright in 1853.[10]

All but two of the Greene-Macdonald letters printed here were written during the time when Margaret Greene owned Dungeness. The estate, and its unsatisfactory tenant, Mr. Nightingale, was often a subject of these letters, for Macdonald, who was not only a lawyer but something of a land speculator himself, proved a valuable source of professional advice. He may even have visited Dungeness, perhaps while he and his wife Isabella (Margaret Greene's sister) were at Savannah in 1845-6. If he did go, it was not to visit Margaret Greene, for at this time she and her other sister Jane seem to have lived almost everywhere in the eastern United States except on their own property. Was it Jane's delicate health or Highland restlessness that took them from East Greenwich to New Haven, from New York to Philadelphia, from Savannah to Clarksville? Whatever the cause, their wanderings ended sadly. Jane, the youngest of the Clark children, her sister's ward and companion, died in Athens, Georgia, in the autumn of 1849.

[6]B. Vanstory, *Georgia's Land of the Golden Isles* (Athens, Georgia, no date), page 166.
[7]Georgia Archives. Camden County, Wills Book "A". Will of Catherine Miller, January 4, 1815.
[8]Georgia Archives. Camden County, Book "N", page 498. Deed drawn August 1, 1843, recorded August 12, 1843.
[9]See page 45, Macdonald to Margaret Greene, January 1, 1846.
[10]Georgia Archives. Deed drawn November 9, 1853, recorded January 18, 1857. Camden County, Book "P", page 424.

Not long after the death of Jane Clark, the letters of John A. Macdonald to Margaret Greene, for no apparent reason, come to an end. Only one additional letter which passed between them survives, a letter from Margaret Greene to Macdonald, written from New York, in 1863. It may have been the last letter she wrote to him. A year later Margaret Greene also died, in New York at the age of sixty-six.

"I always considered you *a Charming Woman*," John A. Macdonald once told his sister-in-law, "but I did not calculate for all your friends being so." Had there been no Margaret Greene, Macdonald and his wife would very likely have travelled to the United States in search of the well-known benefits of sea-bathing and a "change of air", but it is doubtful if they would have travelled so widely, or met such "charming" company. Macdonald, a lifetime British North American nationalist, did not approve of all he saw and heard among Margaret Greene's "Yankee friends", but he did find much to admire. The "letters of credence" supplied by his wife's sister gave him an opportunity not afforded to many of his contemporaries, the opportunity of seeing America from the point of view of Mrs. Greene's well-to-do, cultured, influential relatives and friends. Macdonald, never one to waste opportunities, used his chance to observe closely the political and social behaviour of his hosts, and what he observed he stored away in his remarkable memory, for use on some still distant day.

Among the letters preserved by Margaret Greene are two from her sister, Isabella Macdonald, written in 1845 and 1848, the only letters she wrote which now exist. They are curious letters, passionate, voluble, almost childish. They are also sad letters, the letters of an invalid, letters that reflect the growing deterioration of her health.

Surely no one was ever less suited to a life of illness and inactivity. Isabella Clark was six years older than John A. Macdonald, but her letters seem the letters of a young girl, full of girlish enthusiasm and affection, and sometimes girlish despair. She could not, would not, hide her feelings. "My own darling precious sister," she wrote in one of her letters to Margaret Greene, "you know how headlong I ever go."

It has always been assumed that Isabella's marriage to John A. Macdonald was one of her "headlong" actions, after the briefest of courtships in the Highlands in 1842, and at Kingston in 1843. It is at least possible, however, that she, with her sisters Margaret and Jane, may have been in North America, visited Kingston, and met Macdonald, well before that time. Certainly such a supposition is given some support by Margaret

Greene's first letter to John A. Macdonald, which does not read as if the three sisters and he were then total strangers. Even if there had been no such earlier meeting, it is plain that the legendary first meeting of John A. and Isabella amid the romantic Highland glens did not in fact occur. Quite clearly, if they first met in 1842, it was, as Margaret Greene's welcoming letter also makes clear, at Douglas on the Isle of Man.

There is almost nothing that can be said with certainty about Isabella's early years, but of most of her married life her husband's letters provide an all too graphic account. It was a tragic marriage, overhung through most of its duration by the expectation of death, made more tragic by actual death, of their first-born son, and of Isabella's younger sister Jane. "I have a strong feeling that our circle will not soon again be narrowed," Macdonald wrote after Jane's death, "the rod cannot be always smiting." But again and again the rod smote and the circle narrowed. Three days after Christmas 1857, almost exactly a month after her husband had attained the highest political office open to him, Isabella's tragic life came to an end. She was forty-eight. She had been married for fifteen years and had been an invalid for fourteen of them. Fourteen years of pain, of prostration, of lethargy induced by opium. Fourteen years of faint hopes, and growing hopelessness.

One of the ways in which family life in the nineteenth century differed from that of our more sheltered age was in its greater familiarity with sickness and death. It was necessary to be prepared, to expect that death would come, often with cruel swiftness. It was necessary to be resigned. Grief, though its nineteenth-century expressions sometimes approached morbidity, was no less genuine, only more frequent.

Illness and death were the common lot of all, but it is difficult not to think that the Macdonalds, Clarks, and Shaws suffered rather more than their share of family sorrow. In 1862, five years after Isabella's death, John A. Macdonald, having lost in turn his father, his son, and his wife, lost his mother also. For her death, like Isabella's, the family had been long prepared. Helen Macdonald had suffered the first of a series of a dozen strokes at about the same time that Isabella had first become ill, and had thereafter gone on cheerfully ignoring all warnings to lead a less active life. Hers was not, of course, an early death – she was eighty-five at the time – but for the family her going was no less significant. She had been the matriarch, the last of a generation.

The Macdonald family papers include no letters written by Helen Macdonald. Despite this lack, her presence is very real, not only because she saved a handful of letters from her famous son, but because she was in many ways the focus, perhaps more accurately the heart, of a close family connection. She was the family's memory, the one who knew and cared about the complex interrelationship of her own people, the Shaws, with the Clarks, Macphersons, and Macdonalds. She was the link between families and generations, the keeper of the family lore. Throughout her life her family, scattered and shattered by time, wanderlust, war, and disease, yet bound by fierce ties of loyalty and affection, was her greatest abiding concern.

She was born in 1777, probably at Dalnavert, but nothing certain is known about her early life. The first record we have is of her marriage on October 21, 1811, to Hugh Macdonald, when she was thirty-four and he was twenty-eight. Between 1812 and 1818, five children were born in Glasgow to Hugh and Helen Macdonald. Of William, the eldest, nothing is known except that he died in infancy. The second child, a girl, was called Margaret, after Helen's mother, and the third, a boy, was given the first name John, after Hugh Macdonald's father, and the second name Alexander, the name of one of Helen's brothers. The fourth and fifth children were named James Shaw and Louisa Jean. James Shaw Macdonald's name was of course that of his mother's father, but it was also, and perhaps more significantly, the name of her brother, James Shaw of Georgia. It is also likely that Louisa, the youngest, was named in honour of the younger James Shaw's wife, Louisa Greene.

Two years after the birth of their last child, the Macdonald family – Hugh, Helen, their children, and Helen's mother – emigrated to Kingston, Upper Canada. Hugh Macdonald's second Glasgow business venture, the manufacture of bandannas, had failed, according to family legend, through the duplicity of his partner.[11] The choice of Kingston as a new centre of operations was probably dictated by necessity. Helen had relatives there who were in a position to help Hugh to get a new start. Her half-sister, Anna Macpherson, with her husband, Colonel Donald Macpherson, and their large family were permanently settled in Kingston. The colonel was possessed of some means and some influence in the community and was able to provide temporary shelter and to set Hugh up in a small shop.

Family misfortune followed Helen Macdonald to the new world. James Shaw's death in the year of their emigration had removed her only

[11]J. Pennington Macpherson, *Life of the Right Honourable Sir John A. Macdonald* (Saint John, New Brunswick, 1891), page 77.

surviving brother. The following year her mother died at Kingston, and in 1822 little James Shaw Macdonald, aged six, died accidentally, as the result of a fall. Other troubles followed them as well. Once more Hugh's business ventures did not prosper; shops at Kingston and at Hay Bay, and a mill at Glenora in Prince Edward County each in succession failed. In the autumn of 1835 Hugh Macdonald, "a gentle and most lovable man", fond of books and dreams, gave up his hopes of wealth. Through another of his wife's relations, Francis Harper,[12] he found a position as a clerk in the Commercial Bank of the Midland District, in Kingston. His withdrawal from business coincided with the coming of age and the beginning of the professional career of his son.

Throughout their marriage it was undoubtedly Helen who provided energy and leadership, who encouraged and goaded her husband in his enterprises, who watched over her promising son through his schooling and apprenticeship. John A. Macdonald was like both his parents. He was easy-going, likable, and a great reader like his father, but he had his mother's energy and ambition, and he resembled her physically more than his father. Helen was tall like her son, with features "of a masculine, massive type" that were inherited by two of her children, John Alexander and Louisa. Both, curiously enough, also inherited her interest in the family and its history.

The wanderings of the Macdonalds ended in 1835 with their return to Kingston, where Helen spent the remainder of her years with her dwindling family. After the marriage of her son in 1843 and that of her daughter Margaret in 1852, her youngest daughter Louisa, who never married, remained at her side. In 1860 the family was reunited, as much as it was ever to be. At "Hazeldell", the house of Margaret's husband, Helen Macdonald spent the last two years of her life with her daughters, her son-in-law, and her grandson. She was stubbornly independent to the end. She did not go to Hazeldell as a dependant but as a tenant, paying a yearly rent, and on the formal understanding that she was to be allowed the use of a carriage for her unmarried daughter, her grandson, and her friends.[13]

Hazeldell, and their next home, Heath's farm or "Heathfield", to which they moved after Helen Macdonald's death, gave the Macdonald

[12]Husband of Wilhelmina Macpherson, Helen's niece. Harper was "cashier" or manager of the Commercial Bank.
[13]Queen's University Archives. Williamson Papers. Agreement between Mrs. Hugh Macdonald and James Williamson, May 10, 1860.

family a welcome degree of permanence. Both Hazeldell and Heathfield were well outside the actual town of Kingston. Heathfield, in fact, was literally a farm. There they lived a tranquil country life, Margaret's and Louisa's constant gardening punctuated by expeditions into the town and by visits from friends and relatives, including the sporadic appearances of John A. himself. Their lives cannot have been entirely peaceful, for both sisters had some of their mother's strength of will, but they were old companions and deeply attached to one another. With the exception of about four years between Margaret's marriage and the move to Hazeldell the sisters spent their entire lives under the same roof.

By 1852, when Margaret was thirty-nine and Louisa thirty-four, it is likely that both sisters had begun to resign themselves to lives of spinsterhood. They had already assumed most of the traditional functions of maiden aunts, anxiously watching over their aged mother, attending at confinements and sick beds and minding whole generations of children. Practical, good-natured Margaret, and Louisa, the serious, independent one, shared a common, familiar family routine. But in that year fate, in the form of a professor of natural philosophy, suddenly intervened.

Margaret Macdonald and James Williamson must have known each other, at least slightly, for some years prior to 1852, but their actual courtship was short and impetuous. It was an uncharacteristic action on both of their parts, but there is nothing to indicate that they ever regretted the step taken in such haste.

At the time of his marriage the Reverend Doctor James Williamson was no longer in the prime of youth. He was seven years older than Margaret, born in 1806. His presence in the family introduced a novel strain. He was Scottish, of course, and Presbyterian, but he came not from a remote Highland village but from the metropolis of Edinburgh, and he was neither soldier nor merchant, but a scholar and divine. His parents were able to provide him with a sound Scottish education, and thereby set him on the path he was to follow all his life. He revealed an early avidity for learning. At the famous High School of his native city he won the first prizes for Latin prose and Greek, and at Edinburgh University, for classics and mathematics and natural philosophy. He went on to the study of theology under the renowned Dr. Chalmers, was ordained, and was minister of two Scottish villages.[14] He was a successful minister. "No one," wrote a Kirk minister for whom he had once acted as assistant,

[14]Henry J. Morgan, *Bibliotheca Canadensis* (Ottawa, 1867), page 394.

14

"kept a better filled church than Mr. Williamson."[15] Though a shy man, he inspired great affection in others, but he may not have been entirely happy in the church. When an opportunity arose that permitted him to serve in a way more congenial to his bookish leanings, he quickly embraced it. In 1842 he crossed the Atlantic to join the faculty of Queen's, the new Presbyterian college at Kingston, then just beginning active operation. Before long he had saved enough of his meagre salary to send for his childhood sweetheart, a girl named Margaret Gilchrist. They were married in Kingston in 1845, but the first Margaret Williamson died after only two years of marriage, very likely in giving birth to their only son, James Gilchrist Williamson, who was born in 1847.

At Queen's James Williamson was able to indulge his interest in science, especially in chemistry and astronomy. He was almost single-handedly responsible for the establishment and operation of an observatory at Kingston, which he nursed lovingly through many years, preparing elaborate astronomical reports which almost no one ever read, and lobbying, sometimes through his brother-in-law, for more and better equipment. He achieved a considerable reputation as a scientific scholar, with a number of learned publications on several subjects to his credit.[16] Despite his bookish preoccupations, his lack of a sense of humour, and his ineptness in campus politics, he was popular with both colleagues and students. Nor was he devoid of ambition. In 1864 he tried unsuccessfully to become principal of Queen's. Finally, in 1876, the year in which Margaret died, he was appointed vice-principal, a post he still held at the time of his own death in 1895.

There are many surviving letters from Sir John A. Macdonald to his brother-in-law, more in fact, in this book, than to anyone else. The Macdonald-Williamson correspondence actually predates the professor's marriage to Margaret, though these early letters, which do not concern the family, have not been included here. John A. Macdonald gradually came to include "the parson" in the affectionate regard which he felt for his mother and sisters. He came, too, to depend heavily on this kindly, gentle scholar as a second father for his son Hugh, the only surviving child of his marriage to Isabella. Professor Williamson and Margaret were never to have children of their own, and James Gilchrist Williamson,

---

[15]D. D. Calvin, *Queen's University at Kingston* (Kingston, 1941), page 73.
[16]Morgan, *op. cit.*, page 395. He wrote, among other things, on saline springs, meteorology, North American water resources, and "the natural and industrial productions of Canada".

who was brought up by his maternal grandparents in Scotland, never joined his father in America, so that it was natural that Hugh should come under their care. Even before Isabella's death, Hugh, the child of a politician and an invalid, had become a kind of family property shared in common. When he was ten, with his aunt and grandmother, he moved to Hazeldell, the house which the professor rented, and there and at Heathfield he spent the rest of his boyhood.

Hugh's father was an important figure of whom he was intensely proud, and whose visits were eagerly watched for. But, as Macdonald's political stature grew, the visits became less frequent. The indulgent father of his childhood became more distant as Hugh grew older, and became, as well, more demanding. All his life Hugh strove to please his father, but he could never, no matter how he tried, be like his father, nor what his father wanted him to be. The professor, better than his father, knew Hugh's strengths as well as his limitations. He was a familiar and reassuring presence, a father for every day, for whom the retiring, rather delicate boy came to have a deep, if unspoken, affection and respect.

The sons of famous men bear the weight of impossible burdens, which they can neither carry nor lay down. No miracle could turn Hugh John into John A., there was only one John A., but Hugh, from childhood to the present, has been measured against the accomplishments of his father, and necessarily, found wanting. Hugh followed both of his father's professions, law and politics, yet he might, had he been the son of a different father, have succeeded better in some other career. A profound shyness and a persistent nervousness in public made the path he chose painfully difficult. He had none of his father's casual, easy, confident skill with people, he lacked imagination, tolerance, quick-wittedness, and a sense of humour; but he had his own virtues, the virtues of a good soldier. He was intelligent, loyal, meticulous, and a little romantic, and he could never shirk what he took to be his duty.

There was never any question of a military life for Hugh, but at an early age he did develop a passion for soldiering. When he was sixteen and a student at Queen's, the Fenian Order, an Irish brotherhood which had blossomed in the United States since its formation there in 1859, decided to liberate Ireland by invading the Province of Canada. In June 1866 some eight hundred Fenians crossed the Niagara River at Fort Erie. They were quickly repulsed and did not return, but the invasion aroused Canadians to a sudden need to defend their borders. Hugh John Macdonald, with some of his schoolmates, enlisted in the nearest available militia unit, the 14th Battalion, Princess of Wales Own Rifles, of Kingston, and spent the summer guarding the St. Lawrence against an invisible enemy. He returned to school, the danger evidently past, but did not forget his first taste of military life. Four years later an even more exciting opportunity arose. An expedition to ensure law and order at the Red River Colony left eastern Canada in early March 1870. With it went Ensign Hugh Macdonald of the 16th Company, 1st Ontario Rifles. Hugh was now a law student, having spent his last two college years at the University of Toronto, graduating in the spring of 1869. He left his law studies with no regret to take part in a four-month journey of very real danger and difficulty, by water and wilderness to Fort Garry. He went with only the most grudging consent on his father's part. (Hugh had asked Sir George Cartier to intercede on his behalf: "One word from you would have far more influence with him than a dozen letters from me.")[17] He went also despite the fact that his father had suddenly become desperately ill.

John A. Macdonald's recovery during the summer of 1870 owed nothing to the presence of his only son. Whether or not he resented Hugh's defection at such a time, he did not approve of his son's long leave of absence from his legal training. Hugh was abruptly summoned home from his "outing".[18]

Disappointed that the Red River force was not to be kept together to form "the nucleus of the Canadian Army" in which he might have served permanently,[19] Hugh resumed his studies. He was called to the bar in 1872 and immediately joined his father's firm. But he soon incurred parental disapproval of a far more serious stripe. In the autumn of 1875 he became engaged to a lady whom John A. Macdonald considered totally unsuitable.

Hugh, like his father and his grandfather before him, had chosen a bride somewhat older than himself. She was also a widow, with a tragic past. Jean King was the oldest of the six children of William A. Murray, a well-to-do Toronto merchant. Her first husband had been a brilliant young doctor, John Lyons King, who died at the beginning of a particularly promising career, leaving her with a baby girl, who also died,

[17]Quoted in *Report of the Public Archives*, 1933 (Ottawa, 1934). Hugh Macdonald to Sir George Etienne Cartier, April 7, 1870.
[18]See page 111, Macdonald to Margaret Williamson, September 23, 1870.
[19]Public Archives of Canada. Cartier Papers, M.G. 27, I, D4, Vol. 2, page 1004. Hugh Macdonald to Cartier, June 28, 1870.

aged three, in 1871. In sorrow Jean, herself only twenty-five, went home to her own family. In time the young widow met one of her brother William's friends, Hugh Macdonald. Before long, despite a difference of religions – she was a Roman Catholic – and despite the strong opposition of John A. Macdonald, they determined to be married.

Macdonald was at first annoyed, and then thoroughly angered, by Hugh's refusal to change his mind about the marriage. Their quarrel ended in a personal and professional separation. At the end of 1875 Hugh left his father's firm, Macdonald and Patton, to seek his own fortune. The illness and death of Margaret Williamson in the spring of 1876 brought father and son together again, though their professional relationship was not renewed until 1878, when Hugh became a partner in the family firm.

Hugh and "Jeanie" Macdonald were married for five years, and had one child, named Mary Isabella but known from infancy as Daisy. With Hugh's consent Daisy was brought up in her mother's faith, both before and after the next in the series of Macdonald family tragedies, the sudden death of Jean Macdonald in 1881.

The death of his wife proved a turning-point in the career of Hugh John Macdonald. The course of his life, so unexpectedly and finally changed, had to be thought out once more. Before the year was out he had decided to make a radical break with the past. In the spring of 1882, in company with thousands of his fellow central Canadians, Hugh moved west. The building of the Canadian Pacific Railway had turned Winnipeg temporarily into a boom town, and there he, Stewart Tupper, son of his father's colleague Sir Charles Tupper, and two other young lawyers founded the firm of Macdonald, Tupper, MacArthur, and Dexter. Good times were soon replaced by long years of bad, but Hugh had come to Winnipeg to stay. He married again, in 1883, this time with his father's entire approval. His new wife, Gertrude Agnes Vankoughnet, was the niece of one of John A. Macdonald's oldest friends, Philip Vankoughnet, Chancellor of Ontario, and of his deputy (as Superintendent General of Indian Affairs), Lawrence Vankoughnet. Her background was also highly acceptable on her mother's side, since her grandfather was Senator Benjamin Seymour, once John A. Macdonald's colleague as member of the Legislative Assembly for Frontenac. In 1884 she presented Hugh with a son, John Alexander Macdonald, the third Canadian Macdonald to bear that name.

In Winnipeg Hugh again found ways to indulge his military bent, first as one of the organizers of the 90th Winnipeg Rifles in 1883, and shortly after on active service during the North West Rebellion of 1885. Though plagued with sore feet and an infected face, he served during the rebellion with courage and distinction, was promoted from lieutenant to captain, and won the respect and affection of his men.[20] He returned to a hero's welcome in Winnipeg before settling down to his neglected practice.

After repeated urgings and much soul-searching, Hugh entered politics in 1891. He was elected to the House of Commons as member for Winnipeg in the general election of that year and was introduced in the House, amidst great applause, by his father. It was, ironically, one of John A. Macdonald's last appearances in the House. Hugh had arrived in Ottawa just in time to be a watcher at his father's bedside, during the Old Chieftain's last battle for his life.

After John A. Macdonald's death Hugh served for a short time as Minister of the Interior in the cabinet of Sir Charles Tupper, but he was unseated in 1896, and willingly left public life. In 1899 he was again persuaded that his party needed him. As Conservative leader in the province of Manitoba he was victorious in a provincial general election, and on January 8, 1900, he took office as Premier of Manitoba, President of the Executive Council, Attorney General, Municipal Commissioner, and Commissioner of Railways. Though he worked hard, driven by a strong sense of duty, he had neither his father's relish for politics nor his knack for political longevity. Less than a year after becoming premier, his political advisers convinced him that his duty again lay in the federal field. He resigned as premier, ran against Sir Clifford Sifton in a Brandon by-election, and was soundly trounced. This time he retired for good.

Great misfortune as well as great happiness marked the later years of his life. His only son, whose health throughout childhood had always been uncertain, did not live to manhood, but died in 1905 when he was not quite twenty years of age. Hugh found a measure of consolation in his work, especially after he gave up the active practice of law in 1911 to become police magistrate of Winnipeg. In this office he took great satisfaction. He became a popular, even beloved, figure on the Bench, known among his clientele as a sympathetic and courteous judge of their transgressions.[21] He was knighted in 1913. He lived to be seventy-nine, and

[20]George P. Macleod, "Sir Hugh John Macdonald", Papers of the Historical and Scientific Society of Manitoba, Series III, No. 14 (1959), page 39.
[21]Ibid., page 50.

when he died in 1929 the Province of Manitoba gave him a state funeral.

When Sir Hugh died without a male heir, the family, the descendants of the little group who had come to Kingston in 1820, virtually died with him. He had been the last living male Macdonald. He was survived by his daughter Daisy, but she already bore another name. In 1929 the Macdonald line was not yet, however, extinct, for Hugh had a half-sister, Mary, the daughter of Sir John A. Macdonald and his second wife, Susan Agnes Bernard, whom he married in 1867.

John A. Macdonald's remarriage, at the age of fifty-two, was sudden and unexpected. After Isabella's death he had settled into a comfortable and apparently contented bachelor state, living in furnished lodgings in Toronto and at Quebec City, and, after the government of the province moved to Ottawa in 1865, sharing rented quarters with his assistant and chief clerk in the Attorney General's office, Hewitt Bernard. He was, of course, something of a catch. At least one admirer, the widow of his old friend Judge George B. Hall of Peterborough, made a determined assault on his defences during this bachelor period,[22] but he preferred independence. "I am now so much accustomed to live alone," he told his sister Louisa, "that it frets me to have a person always in the house with me."

In the late autumn of 1866 Macdonald sailed to England to lead his fellow-delegates in a conference on the federation of British North America. On a December day in London while walking in Bond Street he met, or rather re-met, Hewitt Bernard's sister. Two months later they were married.

The Bernards were from Jamaica. When Agnes was born there in 1836, the family had already been established in the colony for a long time, and had attained a position of prominence. Agnes's father, the Honourable Thomas James Bernard, was a lawyer and planter, and a member of the island's Privy Council. When he died in 1850, the family left Jamaica. Agnes, the youngest, was still at school in England, but two of her brothers, Hewitt and Richard, went north to Canada, and settled near Barrie, Canada West. Agnes joined them and her mother there in 1854.

She was seen by her future husband for the first time in a hotel dining-room in Toronto in 1856. "I thought ... that you had fine eyes,"

[22]Public Archives of Canada. Macdonald Papers, M.G.26,A, Vol. 545, page 257930. Mrs. Hall to Macdonald, December 21, 1860.

Macdonald admitted long after;[23] but they did not actually meet until 1859, a year after Hewitt Bernard became Macdonald's private secretary. They continued to meet on a casual social footing until 1865 when Mrs. Bernard and Agnes decided to move permanently to England. The move proved to be something less than permanent. Two years later Agnes was back in Canada as Lady Macdonald, wife of Sir John A. Macdonald, K.C.B., first prime minister of the Dominion of Canada.

As Canada's first lady, Agnes was a distinct success. If she was not beautiful she was imposing, a handsome woman, tall and slender, who grew increasingly regal in appearance with the years. She enjoyed public and social occasions. She was a gracious, conscientious hostess, as indeed she had need to be, for her husband made it a rule to invite each of his parliamentary supporters to dinner at least twice during each session.[24] Agnes enjoyed this part of her married life greatly, despite her occasional protests about overwork. She liked to manage things, liked to manage Ottawa society, liked to manage her servants and her daughter and the workmen who came frequently to redecorate and remodel her house. Within limits, she liked to manage her husband also, although that was not always an easy matter.

It can hardly be supposed that these two strong-willed people lived in invariable harmony, but in many respects their life together was close to ideal. Both gained much from their marriage. Agnes assumed a task which gave her an outlet for her great energy and enthusiasm and a social position in which she clearly revelled. Her marriage gave her opportunities, too, which she might never have had, especially the opportunity to travel and to do unorthodox things; the opportunity, for instance, to ride through the Rockies on the cow-catcher of a locomotive, and to indulge her passion for literature by writing of her experiences afterwards in a fashionable English magazine.[25] Macdonald, at a time when his public responsibilities were rapidly multiplying, was much in need of the stable, organized home life that Agnes could provide. She gave him protection from the critical, demanding world, she gave him the encouragement and the admiration he needed. And to his great delight,

[23]Sir Joseph Pope, *Memoirs of the Right Honourable Sir John Alexander Macdonald, G.C.B.* (Toronto, 1930), page 334.
[24]Ibid., page 642.
[25]"By Car and by Cowcatcher", *Murray's Magazine*, 1887, pages 222-3. She also wrote on occasion for the *Ladies Home Journal* and the *Pall Mall Magazine*.

37144

after two years of marriage, she gave him a child, a daughter, to whom they gave the sonorous name of Margaret Mary Theodora.

Delight gave way all too soon to dismay. Little Mary was not a normal child. Despite all that medical skill could do, she was never to have complete control of her limbs, never to walk without help, nor be able to take care of herself. For Macdonald her condition was the final family tragedy. He had never, even briefly, been permitted to be a normal husband and father, with a normal, healthy family, but now, at an age when most men are grandfathers, he was to have had a home, a wife, and a child. The gift, so miraculously offered, was imperfect, damaged in transit. And this time the gift was to be the last.

For a long time the despairing parents feared that Mary was mentally, as well as physically, impaired, and it seems likely that her father carried this fear with him to his grave. Mary's physical development was painfully slow, and her parents, worried by her ill health, expected little. Her persistent childishness, as other members of the family soon saw, resulted not from a basic weakness but from being treated as a child by her parents. As her physical capabilities increased, her intelligence seemed to keep pace, until a day came when Lady Macdonald could be certain that her daughter was as capable of making her own decisions as she was herself.[26] Yet despite gradual progress there would always be a limit. She would never be like other people; she would never go to school or play games, she would never dance, she would never have admirers, she would never marry.

Between John A. Macdonald and his invalid daughter there arose a very deep attachment. The letters which they wrote to one another are few, but they are full of affection and the loneliness of separation. Her father's death must have affected her profoundly, and she may well have been glad that her mother decided, a year after Sir John's death, to leave the sad house where together they had passed from "the horror of a great darkness into the sad twilight of resignation".[27]

Macdonald's widow survived him by thirty years, and his daughter by forty-two. During those years they lived mainly abroad, chiefly in England, sometimes in Switzerland, or in a warmer climate for Mary's health, but rarely in Canada. At first they intended to come home soon to Canada, but as time passed Canada seemed somehow less and less at-

[26]Public Archives of Canada. Macdonald Papers, Vol. 558, page 269307. Lady Macdonald to Joseph Pope, June 2, 1910.
[27]Pope, op. cit., page xiii.

22

tractive. Lady Macdonald, created a baroness in her own right after her husband's death, enjoyed English society. Canada was too cold for Mary; she would "do better" in England. In 1900 Lady Macdonald sold Earnscliffe, their old Ottawa home, and with it went one of the few remaining ties with the past. Sir John's former private secretary, the faithful Joe Pope, took care of her Canadian estate and patiently made necessary adjustments to her frequent changes of plan. There was really no reason to go home at all.

After her mother's death in 1921, Mary remained abroad, attended by a series of companions. She lived on, but at last her small physical ability, so slowly acquired, began to desert her. Her hands would no longer obey her. Once more as in childhood, she was forced to dictate her letters. In her last years she lived in a nursing-home near Brighton, on the south coast of England. There, in January 1933, she died at the age of sixty-four.

"Our circle will not soon again be narrowed," her father had once written, long, long before. Yet the circle had always narrowed, like the light from a guttering candle, erratically, spasmodically, until it was only a glow, that lingered, faltered, and, almost unnoticed, disappeared forever.

PART ONE ❧ 1842-1857

All but a few of the letters in Part One refer in some way to the long illness of Isabella Macdonald. In her husband's phrase, she was "like the 'invisible lady' that used to exhibit not 'show' herself". From the sick-bed, her long ordeal cast a constant pall over the family correspondence. There is no doubt that the entire family was deeply concerned about Isabella's health and that her condition was for her husband a constant preoccupation, but, as a reading of these letters only partially indicates, it was by no means his only preoccupation. Whatever Isabella's state of health, life for John A. Macdonald had to go on. Money had to be earned, if for no other reason than to pay for the staggering expense of Isabella's treatments and travels in search of health. He worked hard at earning money, and rose rapidly in his profession. In 1846 he was made a Q.C., giving him, as he told Margaret Greene, "the Mighty right of wearing a silk gown, instead of a stuff one". His expanding law firm became solicitor for two prestigious, and litigious, Kingston concerns, the Commercial Bank of the Midland District and the Trust and Loan Company of Upper Canada. Yet there was never quite enough money to go round. At an early date in his professional career he and his firm began to go gradually deeper and deeper into debt. He always managed to remain optimistic and repeatedly tried to recoup his losses, or, more accurately, to make his fortune in business ventures, usually by speculation in land. He bought and sold city lots in Kingston, farm lands at Napanee, railway lands at Sarnia. Before long his real-estate operations covered a dozen counties in every corner of Canada West. In one transaction alone, in 1852-3, he bought and sold 9,700 acres.[1] He was confident that in a developing country land must make him wealthy. "Things pecuniary have prospered with me," he told a colleague in 1853, "and without exertion I will be next year a rich man." Somehow his schemes never succeeded as well as he hoped. His debts, chiefly to his obliging client the Commercial Bank, continued to grow. Other men made money from the law and from land, but success eluded Macdonald. He had heavier demands on his income than many men and he spent money freely in any case, whether on speculations, conviviality, or politics. There was an additional important factor that affected his ability to earn: he gave far less time than was advisable or wise to his own affairs. In 1843, the year of his marriage, he entered local politics, as an alderman in Kingston. The following year he was elected member of the Legislative Assembly for Kingston. From then on he spent more and more time on a promising and absorbing political career, to the neglect of his other interests. In the beginning, as a mere member, he had time to spare for business, and his first term as a minister of the crown, as Receiver General and as Commissioner of Crown Lands in 1847-8, did not make heavy demands on his energy, but in 1854 he returned to office as Attorney General, a post that involved heavy administrative responsibilities. For all that he presented a casual exterior, Macdonald took the duties of office more seriously than most of his contemporaries. It was not only departmental business, however, that occupied his time. From 1854 he was actually, though until 1856 not officially, the leader of the western wing of the Conservative Party.

His rise in the political world was swift, smooth, and apparently easy. Success after success brought him, at the age of forty-two, to the premiership of his province. Yet success was not gained without effort or without cost. "Politics is a game requiring great coolness," Macdonald once told a colleague. It was a game that he seemed to play light-heartedly, but in fact he possessed "great coolness" and he played the game to win. He worked at politics harder and longer than other politicians of the day. More and more his time – for his law practice, for his investments, and even for his family – was sacrificed to the demands of politics and administration.

He did not want to neglect his family. He even brought his wife and son to Toronto to be with him in 1856-7, but it was not easy for a politician in the Province of Canada to maintain a normal home. The pe-

[1]Macdonald Papers, Vol. 544, pp. 257624-257829. Papers relating to the Pickersgill lands.

culiar political rules of the day demanded not only that a politician should be away from home at the provincial capital, but that the capital itself should periodically pick itself up and move, in an untidy, inconvenient fashion, from one end of the province to the other, giving East and West, French and English, equal time. Originally Macdonald had been one of the lucky ones, living in the first capital, Kingston, but he had barely time to take his place in the Assembly before the first move took place, and he followed the perambulating government to Montreal in 1844, to Toronto in 1849, to Quebec in 1851, and back to Toronto in 1855.

Macdonald travelled a good deal, but not only as a political commuter. He went, as his letters show, to England on holiday in 1842, to New York and New Haven with Isabella in 1844, and on the long trip to Savannah in 1845-6. Twice in 1847, during Isabella's first confinement, he made trips to New York. In 1850 and 1857 he was in England again, the first time on Trust and Loan Company business, the second as Premier of Canada, lobbying for imperial funds for colonial schemes. Always, whether for business purposes or not, a trip was an occasion for family reunions.

These constant travels were not as a rule pleasant – they were more often tedious and sometimes perilous – but they were not unusual for the time. Many people, including other members of the Macdonald family, travelled frequently. Margaret Greene and Jane seem to the reader of the family letters to be always in transit. Isabella's brother John passes through Kingston on his way to the United States. "Loo is at Cobourg." "Margaret is wintering at Quebec." Probably, too, there was much more family visiting and travelling than the letters reveal, for they do not in fact provide a very complete record of family occasions. One such journey at least must have been taken by John A. Macdonald for family reasons. At Christmas in 1857 he returned to Kingston from Toronto to be, for the last time, a watcher by his wife's bedside.

1 FROM MARGARET GREENE

[*Douglas, Isle of Man, February* 1842]
I wrote you my dear cousin a long note & enclosed it (thru' a friend) to Mr. Wilson,[1] as I do not know the address of either of you; & I am not only anxious to thank you for your kind & most welcome note, but also to assure you of the delight your visit will afford my sisters & myself.

I much regret that I am under the necessity of moving from my present apartments, I am in the bustle of packing & leaving Douglas for a farm house three miles in the country. My address is Ballafreer near Douglas, & if you will kindly drop me a line saying what day I may look for you & my dear Mr Wilson I shall be in town to receive you & convey you to our country quarters. I shall also request Mr Moore (the Packet agent who goes on Board at her arrival) to give you every information & assistance, in case you may not be able to write me.

I will ask no questions about those dear to us until I have the happiness of seeing you.

Isabella & Jane join me in the affectionate love with which I am my dear cousin,

yrs faithfully
M. Greene

2 TO MRS. HUGH MACDONALD

My dear Mother   London, March 3, 1842
Some anxiety will exist, I suppose in Canada in consequence of the non-appearance of the Caledonia at Boston in her usual time. As I mentioned in my last we were exposed to the same storm that drove her back, but fortunately for us, the wind tho' blowing a tempest was in our favour. The return of the Caledonia, however is a great disappointment both to Wilson & myself, as it will probably prevent us from hearing from Canada until the end of this month and leaves me in uncertainty as to the period of my return. I have, you see, not left London yet, the sights

[1]Thomas Wilson, a former Assistant Commissary General in the British army, was at this time Montreal agent of the Commercial Bank of the Midland District, the headquarters of which was in Kingston. He was married to one of Colonel Donald Macpherson's daughters, Ann Macpherson. Wilson, one of Macdonald's closest friends, had accompanied him on his first trip to England.

and wonders have kept me busily employed since the 17 february. I have not seen half of them yet, and indeed it would take months to do so properly. So having taken a cursory view of the principal ones, I purpose leaving this on Saturday or Sunday evening for Scotland. I shall stop a day or two at Chester on my way, as Evan[2] who is stationed there, has written me to do so if possible. I shall then proceed to Arbroath, and having spent a few days with Major & Mrs Bruce – I beg their pardon – Gardyne,[3] I shall direct my wandering steps wherever my fancy leads me thro' Scotland. Unless Edinburgh detains me longer than I anticipate, I shall not remain in Scotland more than a fortnight, but shall return to the south and meet Wilson and Evan at Kendal in Westmoreland, where we shall have a roam round the lakes, and then to Oxford and Cambridge. Since my arrival in England, my health has been remarkably good. You would be surprised at the breakfast I eat. Wilson laughs as he sees roll after roll disappear & eggs & bacon after roll. My dinners are equally satisfactory to myself and expensive to the chopman. Harper will tell you what a whole beefsteak is. Now only fancy, my commencing my dinner with a sole fried, with shrimp sauce, demolishing a large steak, and polishing off with bread & cheese & a quart of London Stout. This I assure you is not exaggeration, but I find it necessary to support myself against the tremendous quantity of exercise I take every day. I brought a good many letters to people in London, but have hardly found it necessary to use them, as Wilson and his friends here have put me in the way of seeing every thing and going every where. Mr. Edward Wanklyn who resides in London is very attentive to us. He lives in a very nice style and is a very gentlemanly person, and his wife is one of the sweetest women I ever met with. From ill health she is obliged to live a secluded life, but we always find her cheerful & hospitable. Wilson's sister & brother in law Mr John Wanklyn were here, as I wrote you, for some days after we arrived, and through their means I was lionized every where. I think one of the most delightful days I ever spent was with them at Windsor Castle. Mr Wanklyn obtained from Lord De La Warr an order to see the Queen's private apartments, so we saw all the domestic conveniences of Her Majesty and I can assure you, things are as plain & snug as in the family of a private person. Comfort is in no case sacrificed for magnificence or

[2]Evan Macpherson (1804-75) was one of the sons of Colonel Donald Macpherson. He was a captain in the 68th Regiment.
[3]Major David Bruce Gardyne was married to Catherine Macpherson, Evan Macpherson's sister.

show. The state apartments are usually open to the public & the private ones not shown. In our case however it was reversed. The state apartments were closed, as the paraphernalia of royalty which had been prepared for the reception of the King of Prussia had not been removed. By remarkable good fortune however we slipt in, and saw the whole magnificence of the Royalty of England. I shall not attempt to describe the fairlies as they will form the subject of a great many conversations when I return. In one of Scott's novels, he speaks of the unrivalled scenery of Windsor, and certainly the prospect from the terrace opened to my eyes a view which I could not before conceive. I saw it under favourable auspices — The day was clear, the weather warm, and I had a very pretty girl Margaret Wanklyn on my arm, to whom the scene was also new, so we were agreeably engaged in comparing our impressions. Our ideas *sympathized wonderfully*. The engraving of Windsor Castle from the Albion is a very correct one but gives an inadequate idea of the extent & magnificence of the most splendid royal residence in the world. Theatricals I have seen again & again, together with a countless number of exhibitions of all sorts & sizes. At every one of these places I have purchased a catalogue *raissonné* or descriptive account of the exhibitions— These I will bring with me, even to the very play bills – so that you will have every opportunity of tracking my progress thro' the capital.

I have formed acquaintances & dined with two or three lawyers here, by whose assistance I have seen all the great guns of the law. Indeed I have been lucky in all my sight seeing. The first time I went into the House of Lords, they were sitting as a court of appeal and there I saw the 4 great Law Lords, Lyndhurst, Brougham, Campbell & Cottenham. At Guildhall I saw Lord Denman & Sir Nicholas Tindal presiding over jury trials and when I went to the House of Commons I heard speeches from Peel, Goulburn, Lord John Russell, Lord Stanley, OConnell, Duncombe Wakley, Sir James Graham, and most of the leaders in Parliament. I go to day to the Tower & the Tunnel and dine this evening with Harper's old friend Mr Stooks, who has invited two members of Parlt to meet us. The Queen is at Brighton & the Duke of Wellington at Strathfieldsaye So I have not seen either, nor do I now expect to do so until my return to London. I have formed, thro' a kind letter from Hitchings a very desirable acquaintance with a young lawyer named Leach (a nephew of Sir John Leach late Master of the Rolls) who has been of great assistance to me. Notwithstanding all this however, I feel oftentimes a yearning for home & an uneasy desire to be at work. To a person obliged during all his life to be busy, idleness is no pleasure and I feel assured I shall return to my desk with greater zest and zeal than ever. At Manchester I am going to purchase a quantity of damask, an iron railing for the house and a kitchen range. Paper hangings and some chimney ornaments I shall buy here and send all out by Quebec. By the bye I am going to a Bachelor's Ball at Manchester on the 30th. Will Wanklyn, Wilson's oldest nephew is a manager & has given me a ticket and sent one to Evan. The cab is waiting to take us to the City, for you must know we live in the *west* end. So I must close my yarn. Love to Moll & Louisa & to all friends, and believe me ever to remain,

your affectionate son
John A. Macdonald

3 ISABELLA MACDONALD TO MARGARET GREENE

Kingston, June 11, 1845

I put off writing till to-day dearest sister till I would be able to say something decided about our movements. John started for Toronto last evening. But before he went it was determined as no danger is apprehended for dear Mother[4] that we should leave this for New Haven immediately on his return, wh. he at present expects to be on 21st though from last year you will remember he cannot be certain. He is to return at all events, as soon as possible, & as soon as we have any idea of the day we leave this, you shall be written to dearest sister. In the meantime he begged with his best love that you would find out if Irish Margt. could be engaged to attend me while at N.H. If not I must take a servant from here, for you know I said last year I was very determined dear Magt. should not again suffer as then on my account & told John that long before her mother was ill, wh. wd. of itself have put it out of the question altogether. If Irish Margt. leaves aunt M.[5] & can come, I shd. *hope* we would require her *very* early in July, indeed among its first days, but I cannot say how soon till our time is fixed on, & of course I cd. not ask

---

[4]Mrs. Hugh Macdonald, whom Isabella also refers to as "Mama" in this letter, had just suffered the first of her series of strokes.
[5]"Aunt M." was Anna Maxwell, the former Anna Greene, a half-sister of Margaret Greene's late husband. She was married to William Peter Maxwell of East Greenwich, Connecticut.

her to wait if another situation offered. When is her time out with aunt M? & when could she come on to New Haven? I fear there is no chance of getting on at the Sheltons,[6] poor people I am sorry for them, I wish the boarders would take wing just before we arrive. If you cannot *coax or frighten* them let her coax Mrs. McCraggie to take us in. I hope yr next letter will tell me *how* you wish me to lay out the rest of yr portrait money. Jane was thinking of Charly & forgot to specify the articles & I dont know if M. gave my message begging you wd both say what you wished from here. I of course have countermanded yr bonnet dearest sister. But it was to have been lovely. An exquisite lavender satin & blonde but you shall do penance in yellow stockings for it as I thought it wd have been so becoming & sweet. Jane shall shall [sic] wear her *purple* if it *were at night* – for I wont let *her* off. Bye the way Mama has bought a London cap to send you Mrs Abbott had just received it when M. saw & pounced on it. But I am so mad about the bonnet I wont tell what it is like, & I dont think I'll be satisfied till I get a red petticoat for you to wear with the yellow stockings. But seriously I wish you wd let me know what you want from here as getting you anything always puts me in *good humour*. Maria[7] thank God looks remarkably well & says she is so. I'll give her yr message. But as to her writing —— I bought a beautiful Rutland Straw with a wreath of flower for little Joanna a few days ago, & our Aunt did the same for Annie.[8] I am thank God, *much* better, but my head is very confused & I am not sure what I say, only I know I grumble about lavender satin & blonde. Mama is nicely again & may we feel the blessing. But Oh! God, it was dreadful to see her face so twisted. Loo is at Coburgh, *we have heard nothing of her since she left*. How would you like that? I am now going to abuse Jane, But must first say I have received my Martineau & yrs of 4th. Truly & deeply do I grieve that our darling Wm must again go to sea.[9] May God of His mercy watch over him & guide him. I was so in hopes something else wd offer. But He whose Eye takes in Time & Eternity – whose will is ever Wisdom & Mercy, has ordered otherwise. Let us pray His blessing may follow. Miss St. John's death I also grieve for. Oh! those poor children again they are orphans.

[6]Margaret Greene was then living at a boarding-house kept by a Mrs. Shelton of 97 State Street, New Haven.
[7]Maria Macpherson, Isabella and Margaret Greene's sister.
[8]Johanna and Anna Maria Macpherson were Maria's daughters.
[9]William Clark, brother of Isabella and Margaret Greene, was then serving in the Royal Navy. He later entered the service of the East India Company.

The conduct of the Stewarts amazes me.[10] I hope John[11] will be firm & that you may soon hear if the poor little lambs are to come to you. I am sure they will. As for Mr Nightingale[12] there is no *unintentional mistake* about the cotton & much much I fear you my darling sister will suffer. I find I must leave Jane's abuse to dear Margt this time. I hope you'll catch an arrow from her quiver also. Don't you want Flannel? Adieu God bless you both my darling sisters—

MARGARET MACDONALD TO MARGARET GREENE

I have been commissioned by Isabella to finish off your dress my dear Mrs Greene with a gypsy hat and also to abuse Jane, but I will defer the pleasure of scolding Jane until we meet as I cannot write half so fast as I can speak, and shall proceed to touch on matters of rather more consequences. Isabella read your last letter to me that passage in which you speak of my not being able to accompany her on her journey on account of my Mother's health was read with the rest and I rejoiced in hearing it as it broke the ice and enabled me to speak plainly on a subject that I had long been occupied with but on which John and Isabella never touched, viz that of accompanying her to the States. Up to the time of Mamma's attack I looked forward to spending this summer like the last if Isabella consented to going to the States but since that period I feel the greatest reluctance at remaining so far from home as the attack Mamma had was accompanied by strong symptoms of paralysis. Disorders of this kind at all times alarming but particularly so when Mamma's age is taken into consideration, the Dr says that no danger need be apprehended if she will be careful but I regret to say that she will not take the medicine ordered for her. Now that her alarm has passed away, you will not I hope,

[10]One can only guess at the identity of Miss St. John and the orphans. It seems most likely that the orphans were the children of Isabella's oldest brother, James Clark, an army officer who died in 1838, that Miss St. John had been caring for the children, and that the Stewarts were James Clark's in-laws.
[11]John Clark (1798-1864), still another of Isabella's brothers. Like his father and brother, John Clark was a soldier. He entered the British army in 1814 and was at this time lieutenant-colonel of the 54th Regiment. He retired from active service in 1849, but served as commandant of the Royal Military Asylum at Chelsea, 1852-57, and was promoted major-general in 1858.
[12]For a statement of Phineas M. Nightingale's indebtedness to Margaret Greene, see below, pages 43-6, Macdonald to Margaret Greene, January 1, 1846.

my dear Mrs Greene impute my unwillingness to remain with Isabella to an alteration in my feeling of affection towards her but to the real cause my fears for my mother, perhaps they may be groundless but who can tell. Louisa is much better but has suffered more in the last winter than I have ever observed but at our particular period, in the course of her life, she goes on resolutely obeying the doctors orders and reaping the benefit of her obedience. She went to Coburg on Monday and will remain there ten days. To return to Isabella your letter lead to a conversation last night between us she would not listen to my going or remaining with her I said I would not offer to remain but it was my most earnest wish to be with her until she was placed in your care, at first she would hardly allow me speak but I persistedly pointed out as forcibly as I could her inability to take care of herself and poor John however willing nearly as useless as a child I think I have gained her over and I can assure you it will not be my fault if she goes alone. If it should please God to send her health and strength she shall not need any attendance but that of her husband on her return but if it is otherwise ordered I shall with pleasure go with John to take her home.

I have written so hurriedly that I am not sure I have said all I wished if not I hope it will occur to me when I write again. Love to Jane and believe me

ever yours
M.M.

4 To Margaret Greene

My dear Sister   *Kingston, July 11, 1845*
On this day last year, we left Kingston for New York but I fear it will be sometime before we can hope to do so this year. Isabella has been ill – very ill – with one of her severest attacks. She is now just recovering and I hope has thrown off for the time her terrible disease. Still this is not certain, and at all events it has left her in the usual state of prostration that follows every attack. It may be days – nay weeks – before she has rallied sufficiently to attempt any journey. What to say or do, I know not. The summer is wearing away, and may have nearly terminated before the invalid can be moved.

We shall leave this, the moment she can safely become a traveller, and must be guided by circumstances as to the period of our stay in New

Haven. I should think it likely that Dr Knight would send her further south during the winter – and this must be done, tho' I know that Isabella would be much opposed to a separation for all winter.

All the rest of our household are well, as are Maria & her little ones, &c &c &c. Pray give my love and a kiss to Jane, & believe me

ever yours most affectionately
John A. Macdonald

I write in the greatest hurry—

5 TO MARGARET GREENE

My dearest Sister—   Kingston, July 12, 1845

When I wrote yesterday, I expressed my belief that the crisis of her present attack was past. It is so indeed my dearest sister in one sense, her pain has in a great measure left her, but her debility is in the greatest possible degree alarming. She is weaker than she has ever yet been, and there are symptoms, such as an apparent numbness of one limb, and an irregularity in the action of the heart, that made me send for Dʳ Sampson, altho against Isabella's wish. He saw her this morning and says he cannot relieve her, and I ought not, my beloved sister, to disguise from you, that he thinks her in the most precarious state. I would not write thus plainly to you, did I not know your strength of mind, & the impropriety of concealing anything from you. I do not therefore hesitate to tell you, that unless God in his infinite mercy works an immediate change for the better, it is impossible for her to remain in her exhausted state for many days. I send this letter by Oswego, in order that it may reach you more speedily, than by the mail route, but I shall, to prevent mistakes write also by mail.

God bless & protect both of you my beloved sisters and enable you to meet the impending anguish with fortitude & resignation.

John A. Macdonald

6 TO MARGARET GREENE

Oswego, July 18, 1845.

We arrived here this morning about one oclock my dearest sister. The exhaustion produced by carrying Isabella down to the boat, was

35

dreadful to witness. We thought she would die on the deck. We had risked everything however, on the chance, and though sorely tempted to return, we remained on board.

The weather was so stormy, that all our party were sick, Isabella dreadfully so, and yet strange to say her health and strength seemed to return to her, and here we now are safely landed and lodged at the Welland House. Margaret & Louisa are with us. Isa is of course much fatigued with the journey, but is stronger in appearance and pulse than the moment before we left my house at Kingston. We shall remain here, at all events until Monday, and longer if she is not prepared for a journey towards Syracuse. Margaret will write you tomorrow or next day. We join in our loves.

Ever most affectionately yours
John A. Macdonald

7 To Margaret Greene

My dearest Sister   *Philadelphia*,[13] Oct. 31, 1845.

After our parting on Tuesday evening we got safely over to the American House in Jersey City. The stairs were narrow, and *Ishpal* (is that the Celtic mode of spelling?) suffered a good deal before she got to her couch. The perfect quiet of the house & streets was very refreshing to her after the noise of the city hotel, and she soon rallied, & was as comfortable as could well be expected. We remained there all Wednesday & yesterday morning started for the Quaker city. Her fatigues were very great and she was obliged to subdue pain by opium, but still she kept up her spirits & about four oclock we arrived at this House. Only think what a journey she had. First to be carried down a narrow stair at Jersey & over to the cars; 2^d a journey in the cars for about 70 miles to Bristol 3^d. To be carried in a chair from the cars to the steamboat 4th a voyage of 22 miles to this city & lastly and worst of all a quarter of a mile's drive in a hack over the rough streets here. It was enough to fatigue a convalescent, & was fearful for a confirmed invalid. I am delighted to see her bear it so well, for she from fatigue & opium combined, slept from 10 oclock last night until the morning, and is now easy and in good

[13]The Macdonalds were now en route from New Haven to Savannah, Georgia, where Isabella was to spend the winter.

spirits. She never speaks of it, but I am perfectly conscious how much she suffers from being away from you, & without the aid of your untiring and judicious attentions, which were always at hand by night & by day when needed.

However Annie[14] and I do our d——dest (as the Methodists say) to make her comfortable, and I hope & believe, that notwithstanding our awkwardness, Isa's returning vigour will enable her not only to endure, but to profit by the journey.

We have secured a comfortable & quiet room and as the people of the House are civil & attentive, we shall here remain until Monday morning when, God willing, we will leave at eight oclock for Baltimore, by the cars. We will arrive there about three in the afternoon, so you see, we think ourselves pretty strong, when we calmly make up our minds for so great a draft on our strength. Isa sends bushels of love to you and Jane, and is anxious to hear about you and how you are, and how you bore your journey and how Jane's cold is, and how Uncle & Aunt Maxwell is, and how Jane behaved to Mr Kennys when they parted at New York &c, &c, &c. It would be useless for you however to write to us while en route, but we will expect to find all kinds of correspondences waiting us at Savannah.

I shall write you on Sunday evening, reporting progress. Meanwhile with all sorts of love to yourself & Fenella, believe me

ever yours most affectionately
John A. Macdonald

Fragment of an old ballad found in the reticule of a lady— The lady unknown, but the handkf was marked J.G.C.

"How I love Dear William Kenneys
"I will press him to my heart
"And by & bye I'll hem his—
"Dickeys all so smart".

8 TO MARGARET GREENE

My dearest Sister   *Philadelphia, Nov. 3, 1845.*
Isabella was very tired all Friday, as you may imagine, but hoped everything from her nights rest. Unfortunately her rest was disturbed,

[14]Probably a servant.

and on Saturday morning she was unrefreshed. During the day she was visited by your friend Mrs. Biddle, and exerted herself too much, so that in the evening she was a good deal exhausted, and was threatened with tic so that she had recourse to opium. It rained all night and all Sunday, and she felt out of sorts & uncomfortable all day. She slept a good deal during the afternoon but not much during the night. This morning the weather was unsettled & damp, and Madame Isa still felt uncomfortable, so we have stayed over. Tomorrow we hope to leave here without fail. She has had a good day today, has walked a good deal & eaten pretty well, and if she only has a good night, will be bright as need be tomorrow.

I was asked to Mr Biddle's on Friday evening but did not like to leave Isabella. On Saturday evening however, I was seduced from my allegiance to my Petticoat Government by Mr Robinson who took me to a conversazione of the Wistar Club at Dr Randolphs, where I met all the Science & Belles Lettres of Philadelphia.[15] I was much gratified by the feast of Reason, but I say it with shame & confusion of face that my supper of terrapins and champagne lingers more pleasingly on my recollection, than all the "wise saws and modern instances" that were uttered by the savans. Like the apostles my spirit was willing but my flesh was weak & required those creature comforts. It rained so tremendously yesterday that I was prevented from going to church, and as they say in Galway, "I made mee Sowl" at home. Today after a saunter thro this city of marble steps, broad brims & scrubbing brushes, I called on Mrs Biddle whom I found at home. I like her self possessed English manner very much. She is a ladylike & intelligent person and I regret having had so small an opportunity of knowing her. Mr Biddle I was not fortunate enough to meet, but his son Thos called & him I saw. Tell Jane that W^{ms} Biddle is about to leave her "All alone for to dee" & to take a yf to himself. Break it to her cautiously my dear Sister, for fear of consequences.

I forgot to tell you that Mrs Robinson, a sweet pretty woman called

[15]This letter provides some indication of the kind of American society in which Margaret Greene, by virtue of her marriage, moved. Some of the prominent Philadelphians whom Macdonald met through her and who are mentioned here were: Thomas Biddle, a Philadelphia business man, and his wife and sons; Thomas A. and Jonathan Williams Biddle; Moncure Robinson, a famous engineer (the builder of the Philadelphia and Reading Railroad); and Dr. Jacob Randolph, a leading Philadelphia surgeon and professor of surgery at the University of Pennsylvania. The Wistar Association to which Macdonald was taken was a learned society which met weekly to discuss literary, scientific, theological, or philosophical topics.

on Saturday, & I went to find her out to day, but the directory was vague & I was stupid, & so I did not see her again, much to Isabellas delight, who says she does not like my taking so much to your lady friends. By the way, sister there is a latin proverb *"Noscitur a Sociis"* which may be translated for the benefit of the country members, "birds of a feather flock together". I always considered you *a Charming Woman*, but I did not calculate for all your friends being so. From those I have seen, I have only to say, that you will confer a great favor on me by sitting down & writing me letters of credence to *every one* of your Yankee lady friends, and it will go hard but I deliver most of them. I hope Jane has recovered her health & spirits, & found *some* beaux left at Rhode Island. Tell Aunt Maxwell I am resolved to take her by storm, some day or other. I am resolved too, that she *shall* like me & be good to me, & give me some of that ginger bread, that I only got a taste of. Just enough to make me like Oliver Twist "Ask for more". With Love to Jane I remain D͏ͬ sister,

yours most truly
John A. Macdonald

P.S.   I say like Jeanie Deans in her letter to Reuben [Bullen] "Excuse spellin' & ritin' as I hae an ill pen"

9 TO MARGARET GREENE

My dear Sister–   *Baltimore, Nov. 7, 1845*
     Our journey from Philadelphia was a most fatiguing one. The carriage down to the cars & the annoyance we experienced in crossing the Susquehannah was bad enough, but on our arrival in this city, we faired worse. We were promised good rooms on the first floor at the U.S. Hotel, the one nearest the railway, & which for that reason I chose, but on going into the house found we were deceived, and had to make a second move hither. The consequence of all this was great exhaustion & great suffering by Isabella. She was in great agony all night & the two following days, and was obliged to have recourse to opium, externally and internally, in large quantities. She had rather a better night of it last night, and thinks herself able to take her pilgrim's staff in her hand to day. Should she continue well during the morning – we purpose leaving this in a steamer at 4 P.M. for Norfolk, going down Chesapeake Bay & arriving there at 6 in the morning. We are there transferred to a James

River Steamer, which takes us to within 7 miles of Petersburg. There we intend resting for a time to recruit, & from that point, there is railroad communication direct to Wilmington. Should the Chesapeake be calm, of which there is every appearance, we will be able to glide along without the fatigue attendant on the railroad route & its frequent changes.

From Wilmington we go by steamer to Charleston & thence to Savannah, where Isa will try the effect of a Georgia climate, & exercise on its sands. On our way hither a lady was very kind to Isabella & lent her a most comfortable pillow, & when we compared notes we found the lady to be an old friend of yours, Mrs McAlister from Savannah.

Isa sends her warmest love to yourself and Jane, and says she does not anticipate suffering from our todays journey, as the weather is calm. When shall I see you again? I feel quite at a loss for the want of my peaches & milk, & those other little delicacies you were wont to prepare for me at New Haven.

Ever most affectionately yours
John A. Macdonald

10 TO MARGARET GREENE

Wilmington Nov. 15, 1845

Our stay at Petersburgh, my dearest sister, was as comfortless as could well be imagined. The house where we stayed was dirty, the food badly dressed and the beds overrun with ants. You may therefore be sure that Isabella did not gain much there, and on Monday afternoon last, we departed nothing loth, by the cars for Weldon. At that place containing some eight or ten houses, we at least found cleanliness, civility and quiet.

Isabella occupied herself in recruiting, and I in wandering along the banks of the Roanoke, so famous in Virginian Story. Annie discovered in someway or other, the identical stone on which Captain Smith's head was laid, when Pocahontas saved it from the war club of her father. I was very anxious about this part of our journey, i.e. from Weldon to Wilmington, as it was the most tedious & disagreeable of all. We were obliged to leave at night, there being no day line & travel all night, and so on Thursday evening Isa feeling pretty well, buckled on her armour, and at two oclock, was carried down to the cars. The distance hither is one hundred and sixty miles and it was nearly one oclock yesterday before she was landed at our present abode. There was only one stopping place on the road, but Isa preferred continuing the journey. She bore it like a *Shero* as she is but was as you may well believe, dreadfully exhausted by the exertion. She passed a miserable night and continues today to pay the penalty for her extra exertions, but we hope that a quiet night & tomorrow's rest will set her up again.

Our purpose is, God willing, to take the Charleston Steamer here on Monday at noon, which arrives at that place on Tuesday morning at six oclock whence, should Isa be well enough, we will at once be transferred to the steamer for Savannah and arrive at our journeys end that same evening. In all probability, therefore, my next letter will be dated from Savannah, and we will have time to rest and recruit after the most anxious & comfortless journey either my *cara sposa* or myself have ever undertaken. My letters at Savannah will probably enable me to decide on the time of my return, of which I will duly apprize you. Meanwhile I will take all the necessary steps to make my poor sufferer comfortable for the winter.

The house we are now honoring with our presence is no great thing, but the people seem obliging and the house tolerably quiet & clean. The owner rejoices in the warlike name of "Battle" which is rather a misnomer, as he is a messenger of peace as a Methody preacher. Thus you see he supplies aliment for soul and body. Since our journey we have been reading a good deal – & on thinking of what books, we have dipped into, they certainly form a strange melange – to wit – Tom Burke, The Bible in Spain – Rookwood – Carlyle's Life of Schiller, & Bishop Moore's Sermons. We are about to take up Lord Mahon's History of England from the Peace of Utrecht to that of Aix-la-Chapelle, which is written in an impartial & amusing style.

We are in great expectations of finding a budget of letters for us at Savannah. We are hungry for news, having been without any communication with our friends for three weeks.

Isa & myself write in warmest love to Jane & yourself.

Ever yours most affectionately
John A. Macdonald

17th Isabella was very unwell all yesterday, but says she is much better to day. She is evidently not got round yet, but insists in going on, as the weather is very fine & the day calm & mild. We leave about noon.

My dearest Sister–   *Savannah Nov. 20, 1845.*

Tired of the filth, noise & annoyances inumerable of the Franklin Hotel, Wilmington, Isabella, though by no means fit to encounter a voyage, resolved to attempt it. On Monday at noon we accordingly found ourselves gliding down the Fear River in the good steamer Gov.ʳ Dudley. The day was fine, and she – (Ishpal not the steamboat) was comfortably placed in the ladies saloon. There was scarcely a curl on the sea when we reached it, and it continued in one of its most amiable moods. A child might "lay its hand upon its mane", until our arrival at Charleston about seven next morning. Isa was, as you may well suppose, a good deal exhausted by so long continued an exertion, but still preferred going on without delay to Savannah. We therefore transferred ourselves to a steamer, and arrived at this city of sandy streets, and circular squares on Tuesday night about ten oclock. We at once drove up to this house in a "bus", and were fortunate enough to obtain without delay two quiet rooms in the rear of the basement story. We are here at last therefore after many perils by land and water, and gladly look forward to a season of rest. Isabella has been very miserable ever since our arrival. The tic encouraged by her weakness from fatigue has made a furious attack upon her, which she is *manfully* resisting with the assistance of the blister and pill box. I trust that as her fatigue leaves her, so will her persevering enemy, and that my next letter will convey to you accounts of her returning energy & health. Yesterday morning Mr Burroughs & his son Berrien called on us, and we were sorry to learn that Mrs. B. was very ill indeed from cold & confined to her room. In the evening I accompanied them to a Whig meeting & had the pleasure of hearing Judge Berrien[16] speak for about two hours. He is evidently an able man, with great fluency and force of expression, but has the great fault of American speakers (with, I believe the single exception of Webster) of being too theatrical in his manner, & turgid in style. The great proof however of eloquence, is the successful impression made on the minds of the auditors, and judged by that criterion, Mr Berrien's oratory is perfect for nothing could be more enthusiastic than the greetings of the audience. Afterwards I went up to Mr Burroughs house, and got a taste for the first time, of some peach brandy.

[16]John Macpherson Berrien (1781-1856), United States Senator for Georgia, 1824-9, 1841-52, Attorney General of the United States, 1829-31.

We found three of your letters waiting us at the post office, which were most welcome, after our long abstinence from news from friends & home.

I am much obliged by your kind introductions of which I shall be happy to avail myself.

As yet I have taken no steps towards getting rooms at a boarding house, but intend to go to Mrs Hardy's[17] tomorrow or next day & see whether Isa can be made comfortable there for the winter. I hope it will not interfere with your plans, to come south this far, if so, do not on any account do it. Isa is now fretting herself with the idea that you will forget & neglect your own interests & feelings on her account. I need not say however that it would afford me great pleasure to reflect that you were near her, when I am far away, among the frosts & snows of Canada, sucking my paws like any other bear. I cannot delay my departure much longer, which must take place about the beginning of the month. I have yet however fixed on no precise day. Tell Jane that all she wants to restore her is to sit on my knee for a little. My nursing will do her as much good as homeopathy has done her evil.

The weather here is so fine & warm that I cannot fancy it winter at all. If one had only plenty of money? I should like much to spend one *warm* winter, but such must not be & I must return to the *cold comfort* of Canada again. With love to Jane & yourself from Isa & myself I am D^r sister   most faithfully yrs
                                                         John A. Macdonald

12 TO MARGARET GREENE

My dear Mrs Greene   *Savannah Jan. 1, 1846*
    I have made a rough estimate of your account against Mr Nightingale with interest up to this date. This account includes your annuity due this day, and the interest on the $6000 being the purchase money of Dungeness. I observe that no interest has been paid you on this last mentioned sum since you gave Mr. N. credit for it on your decree, and I should decidedly recommend that you will not allow this interest to run in arrear, but insist on his paying up the amt now due say $1037, and regularly continuing to do so. His own estimate of the value of the Dungeness property is $7,000, and as your claim with interest now

---

[17]Isabella was installed shortly after at Mrs. Hardie's boarding-house.

exceeds that sum, you are every day losing by continuing to hold the property.

Mr Law, whom you will of course consult, before doing anything, agrees with me that you should not permit this interest to accumulate.

On considering the whole matter, I would advise

1st That your deed be *forthwith* registered, and the title made indubitable.

2[d] That you should get Mr Law to give the notice required according to your agreement, in order to enable you to sell Dungeness absolutely and without incumbrance

3[d] Should Mr N. omit to pay up the interest on the $6000, that you should sell Dungeness immediately on expiration of the notice. If he pays up the interest regularly, you, I suppose will have no desire to sell the place, against Mr. N.'s wishes.

4th If Mr. N. omits to make the delivery of the 50 bales agreed on, you will, I presume, be obliged to appoint an agent to make a demand therefor, in Baker County[18] as the agreement specifies that they are to be delivered to you or your agent in that county.

5. In case of default in delivery of these bales, you have, as you are aware, the right to proceed at once for the collection of the whole balance due you, but it appears to me that it would not be prudent in you to do so, so long as you find Mr. N. desirous of fulfilling his contract in good faith— I think however that he should in fairness allow the proceeds of the cotton to be applied in liquidation of your current annuity in the first place, and the balance only, if any, should be applied on the decree. By the present agreement these proceeds are to apply in payment of the decree, so that it will in a few years be paid off, and your remaining claims against him, will be for the arrears of your annuity for which you will have no security, by way of judgment or otherwise.

If Mr Law thinks well of it, I would advise you to insist on a settlement being made on the terms above specified. It can make no difference to Mr. N. whether the proceeds are applied on the decree or on your annuity, & it is of the greatest consequence to you.

I do not think of any other suggestions just now, but I will conclude by pressing on you the necessity of not taking any steps in the matter, however trivial without reference to your legal adviser.

Ever yours most sincerely
John A. Macdonald

[18]Baker County is in south-western Georgia.

Decree in equity agt. Mr. Nightingale $14013.89–
          Int from 11 April 43 to 9 Novr 1843 at,   654.00
          which time deed for Dungeness was given $14667–89
          By purchase money of Dungeness_____   6000.00
                                                       $ 8667 89–

PM Nightingale Esq
          In acct with Margt Greene–
1843
Novr. 9– To balance of decree in equity _____ $ 8667.89–
1844
Jany 1   " annuity due this day._____   1000.00
1845
Jany 1   " Do   Do   Do_____   1000.00
1846
Jany 1   " Do   Do   Do_____   1000.00
                                                     $11667–89
"   "   Int on bal decree from 9 Nov 43 $1483–16
"   "   " on annuity due 1 Jany 44_____   160.00
"   "   " on annuity due 1 Jany 45._____   80.00
"   "   " on $6000 purchase money
"   " of Dungeness from date of deed   1037.00   2760.16
                                                             $14428– 5
          Amt brot over_____
          To amt brought over_____ $14428. 5.

                              Cr

1843
May   By Cash from self   150–00.
          Interest   32–00–
Dec   4   " Cash fr Mr Mackey   100. 00
          Int_____   16. 00
"   "   " Cash for Mr Law   300. 00
          Int_____   49. 80

                    45

1844					
March		" Cash for Self	100. 00		
		Int_____	14. 60–		
June	14	" proceeds on 50 bales	1277. 24		
		Int	157. 50		
1845					
April	24	Check on Fox & Livingston	500. 00		
		Int_____	27. 00		
July	26	– Check in Do_____	700. 00		
		Int_____	23. 50		
			3448. 24		
		My balance____	10979–81	$14428– 5	
1846					
Jany	1.	To balance due this day	$10979. 81–		

13 TO MARGARET GREENE

Kingston Feb. 27, 1846

I am in receipt, my dearest sister, of your kind and welcome letter of the 12th, giving me cheering accounts of my darling wife's continued improvements. We can scarcely expect, that her nerves after being in such a state of excitement, and morbid action for so long should at once sink into a state of quiescence, but I am sanguine in my hopes and belief, that in the fine climate she now enjoys, and under your affectionate and judicious care she may yet be restored to me, in health, strength and spirits. I cannot be too gratified to all Savannah friends for their attentions and I beg that you will in an especial manner tender my heart felt acknowledgements to Mrs Kollock for her kindness in allowing Isa so frequent use of her comfortable carriage.

I am truly glad to learn from yourself, that you too are better. Never be weary of well doing, continue to improve, so that when I next see you, you may be again like your portrait which I see every morning, when first I open my eyes and which carries my thoughts at once to Savannah to Isabella and to you. I am glad to hear of Mrs B'.s good health. I suppose she must shortly be expecting her confinement. I sincerely pray she may safely "Win through wi'it" as Meg Merrilies would say.

Maria and her family are all well, Mrs Lowther well too, but her children are delicate and the damp of her house affects them most injuriously. I am happy to tell you of Evan's great kindness to his two sisters inlaw. He allows Maria & Mrs Lowther fifty pounds each per annum, and this seasonable assistance will enable the latter to procure a more healthy & comfortable dwelling. Is he not generous?[19] When he wrote, he was with his *cara sposa* at Paris, from whence they were to proceed to Switzerland and ultimately during the summer to Naples.

Harper has had a severe fit of the gout which has pulled him down a good deal but he is all right again.

I am much surprised at Mr Law's culpable carelessness in not registering your mortgage & disappointed at his want of candour in not mentioning it to me, when I saw him. I would recommend you to ask Mr De Leon, what the law is in that particular, and should it be the case that the mortgage is rendered void by the omission, no time should be lost in procuring a second one. The first deed probably contains a covenant or agreement, on the part of the seller, for what the lawyers call "further assurance" in which case, you can, I presume, compel her to grant you a new deed. At all events I suppose Mr Nightingale will make no objection to give you a new one. I am sorry that his funds are so low, but I hope that you will not lose sight of the great importance of having the remittances you have received, and are to receive, applied in the *first place* to the payment of your annuity & the surplus only credited on the decree in your favour. Make this a *sine qua non*, & in case of refusal show Mr N. no further mercy, because such a refusal, will irresistably prove his intention not to be honest. Pray pardon my pressing this on you, for I think it but justice to yourself and to Jane. All here unite in love to you & yours. The girls & the young Logies go in the morning to Picton to Mr Grants, as I yesterday wrote Jane. Kiss Isa for me & tell her to kiss you in return as my agent. Dont forget a weenie weenie kiss for Jane & believe me

ever your affectionate brother
John A. Macdonald

[19]Evan Macpherson's sisters-in-law were Eliza (McLean) Macpherson, widow of Lowther Pennington Macpherson of Picton (died 1836), and Maria (Clark) Macpherson, widow of John Alexander Macpherson of Kingston (died 1844).

Kingston Jan. 20, 1847

I received your kind letter, my dearest Sister, and am truly sorry to find that Jane has been suffering since your arrival at Savannah. She stood the voyage – and such a voyage – so well that I hoped a few days rest would have done wonders for her, and I trust that your sunny southern weather will soon set her up again. I hear regularly twice a week from New York, and on the 11th my birth day, poor Isabella sent me a few lines of congratulations in her own trembling handwriting.[20] Altho' very slowly, she is still steadily strengthening and I have yet hopes that skillful treatment directed specifically to the first cause of her illness may restore her to some degree of health. She, poor dear girl, will not allow herself to hope, and perhaps it is only my sanguine temperament that makes me do so. I am glad to find that Dr. Washington has wormed himself into her good graces, which, you know with her is a great deal in favour of the success of his treatment.

I had a fatiguing and unpleasant journey home, which nearly laid me up, but I soon recruited and am well as ever. Busy enough as you may suppose, to make up my arrearages. When I was away Her Majesty was graciously pleased to appoint me one of Her Counsel learned in the law. This gives me the *Mighty* right of wearing a Silk Gown, instead of a Stuff one, & as Queen's Counsel gives me rank & precedence over my brethren. The appointment was made in the most gratifying way – in my absence & without solicitation or expectation on my part of any kind. I have since been offered the Solicitor Generalship which I declined because although it gives little or no trouble, & is worth £600 a year I thought it made me too dependent on Gov[t], and I like to steer my own course.[21] All our friends here are well, and in good spirits Maria's children are really as fine youngsters as I ever saw, & if Maria would only bring them up on some system she would have every cause to be proud of them. And so you are back to Mrs Hardie. Give her my love and tell her how I long to hear her sing, "My Boat is on the Shore" again. As I cannot have that pleasure in person, Jane must be my proxy and listen to it twice a day on my behalf, and as often on her own as she pleases. Poor Mrs Renshaw, you will miss her, as with all her deafness and badinage, she was a kind & ladylike person, and the only *decent* person in the house. If you see Miss Black

[20]Isabella was in New York City awaiting the birth of her first child.
[21]Four months later, on May 21, he accepted office as Receiver General.

pray kiss her for me. I know you like her. I am happy to find you have a prospect of a settlement with Mr Nightingale. Be sure and write me particularly, how you did settle, & if not too long send me a copy of the arrangements. Let all the monies you have received, be applied to the pay^t of the interest on the Dungeness property & on your annuity, which is not included in the decree, in the first place as mentioned in my mem. to you. Present my kindest regards to Mrs Burroughs, her *Caro Sposo* and amiable family— Especially to the *Splurgee*, if he be at home. If you do go to Augusta, I hope Isabella will be able enough to join you in the spring. I know she will object to the lengthened separation but it is our last hope, and it *must* not be thrown away. Kiss my darling Jane again & again for me, & believe me to be as ever, My dearest Margaret,

your affectionate brother
John A. Macdonald

15 To Margaret Greene

New York April 5, 1847

Here am I, my dearest Sister, once more in this American Babylon. When our accounts of Isabella's health became so unfavorable, poor dear Maria at once & cheerfully volunteered to take Margaret's place as nurse, and we arrived here last Thursday, Mamma taking charge of Maria's children in the meantime. We found Isa, considerably better than our fears led us to anticipate, and Maria, who sets herself up as very skilful in these matters, confidently predicts that all will go well. Doctor Washington still says she is in a very critical situation arising from the continued attacks of uterine neuralgia. These attacks, he apprehends, may bring on a premature confinement, and if so, God alone knows, what may be the consequence. Still he is not without hopes of being able to prevent an abortion, and in such case her health will probably be completely restored. Every day passed in quiet, adds to the chances in her favour, and we must hope for the best. She is quite calm & resolute, and is much encouraged by Maria's presence. Margaret became quite frightened and nervous from her not knowing what to do, and lost her usual presence of mind. Isa saw that, and felt a corresponding depression, but Maria's skill, cheerfulness and confidence of a happy issue, has done much to set her at ease. She bids me send you and dear little Jane her warmest love and begs you, on no account to think of coming north for her sake. The removal of Jane just now could not be effected without great risk, and you could do Isa no good. Doctor Washington insists on such perfect quiet, that he will not permit two persons in the room with her at the same time, and if you all were here, he should ask the three sisters, which of them would take Margaret's place as nurse, and the nurse only would have the *entreé* into Isabella's room. Under these circumstances, as she would be debarred from seeing much of you, she feels quite unhappy at the idea of your exposing Jane to the wretched weather of the next two months. I was very sorry to hear of your sufferings and Jane's, & can only hope that the southern spring may renovate you both. I hope you got my letter in answer to yours respecting your arrangement with Mr Nightingale and that you have made a satisfactory settlement.

I had a visit yesterday from Mr Charles Greene who is now with his brother Nathaniel[22]— He sends all sorts of love to Aunt Margaret & Miss Jenny. By the way Isabella charges me with having *cut* Mr Nathaniel Greene. Now I should of all things regret being supposed guilty of such a piece of uncalled for rudeness towards any person, and much more towards a friend of yours. I have no recollection of seeing Mr Greene but once and that was when I had the pleasure of conversing with him in his own office on Beaver St. If I met him at any other time I must either have not seen him at all, or not recognized him. Should he be under the impression that I did act in this way, I beg of you, in justice to me, to write him that I am not conscious of having done so. Maria has not been very well since our arrival. The fatigues of the journey has probably put her a little out of sorts.

Margaret & I return to Kingston in a day or two. With warmest love to Jane & yourself, I am my dear Sister,

Yours most affectionately
John A. Macdonald

16 TO MRS. HUGH MACDONALD

My dear Mother–   *Montreal June 10, 1847*
     I was truly and sincerely grieved by Margaret's letter telling me of your indisposition. I beg of you to keep up your courage. Such attacks

[22]Charles Collins Greene and his brother Nathanael, New York business men, were the sons of Margaret Greene's brother-in-law, another Nathanael Greene.

are not uncommon in the aged people and are of course to be guarded against. These illnesses should have the effect of inducing you to be more particular in keeping your system in order, and conquering your antipathy to medicine.

I shall look with anxiety for another letter from Margaret tomorrow informing me of your being convalescent.

I have not had a single word from New York since I came here, except the scrap sent me by Marg[t] from Kingston, and I am becoming very anxious. Pray let Marg[t] write me whenever she hears from Maria, as I will otherwise get but few accounts about Isabella.

Our House is at this moment making all kinds of speechees [sic] The great struggle for power & place is going on, and it is impossible to say what may be the result.[23] With love to the girls I am my dear Mamma

Your affectionate son
John A. Macdonald

17 TO MRS. HUGH MACDONALD

My dearest Mother   New York August 2, 1847.

Mrs Harper and myself arrived here from Montreal on Saturday morning & found poor Isabella tolerably well & Maria quite bright at our arrival. Isabella became quite unwell yesterday morning and suffered a good deal all day, until about 7 in the evening we were obliged to send for Doctor Washington who pronounced her in labour. She suffered for some hours tremendously, when we called in Doctor Rodgers a phycian [sic] celebrated for the use & application of the *Lethean* or somnific gas. She was too weak & her nerves in too disordered a state to give her enough to set her asleep, but from time to time, enough was administered to soothe her considerably. She suffered dreadfully all night and about 8 this morning was so weak that the Doctors determined to use the forceps, as she was quite unable to deliver herself. They succeeded to a miracle, and I am delighted to tell you that she was delivered of a healthy & strong boy. She is dreadfully prostrated & weak and it would be prema-

[23]The Assembly had opened a week before, with a reconstructed ministry, following the resignation of William Henry Draper, the Conservative leader. The new ministry survived until the next general election in December 1847.

ture to speak of her, but on the whole Doctor Washington says that matters have gone on better than he anticipated, & he hopes soon to see her gain strength. The first word the poor thing said, after being informed that the child was alive, & not deformed, was to tell me to write you, and to ask you to give it a name[24] which in her name & my own, I now do. I shall write you tomorrow or next day at furthest. If I do not write tomorrow think it good news.

Mrs Harper writes to Mrs Greene by today's post. Love to the girls.

Ever your most affectionate son
John A. Macdonald

18 To Margaret Greene

My dearest Sister–   *New York August 31, 1847*
Since I wrote you last Isabella has had occasional returns of pain in her left side & limb for which she has used leeching & blistering up to Saturday last. On Wednesday evening last, poor Dr Washington was with her, but was confined to his bed on Thursday & in the evening sent her word he would try & see her on Friday. He was attacked with inflammation of the bowels, which the doctors were unable to subdue, and he died yesterday afternoon. So long as he retained his senses he insisted on prescribing for Isabella, & had Lizzie brought to his bedside twice a day to hear her report. He had transferred all his other patients to Dr Parker. Isabella had a very comfortable day on Sunday, but yesterday morning as she felt the pain returning, I would not allow her continue the treatments of leeching, and insisted on calling in another physician. She was very unwilling to do so, so long as Dr Washington was in life, but I was resolute, & called in a Dr Johnston who stands very high here, and was strongly recommended to us by several of our friends.

He has in some degree changed the treatment but of course, as yet, has not determined on any distinct course to adopt. He has seen her twice & will see her regularly in future.

We have only heard once about Baby since he left us. He was then well. I presume he was quite well 4 hours ago, as we have a telegraph now to Kingston & any illness would at once be communicated to me. I shall

[24]The child was called John Alexander.

52

write to Maria to send you a lock of his hair, which is at present exactly of the colour of his Mother's. His eyes are dark blue, *very large & nose* to match. When born his length was 1 foot 9 inches & was strong & healthy though thin, but as Maria told Dr Washington, that was not to be wondered at, seeing he had been living on *pills* so long. I shall remain here until the Doctor declares Isabella convalescent. Our future course can only then be determined. With united love to Jane & yourself, I am my dear sister,

most affectionately yours
John A. Macdonald

19 To Margaret Greene

My dearest Sister—   *Montreal Sept. 28 1847*
I have been very much occupied since my return here, and you must therefore pardon my not writing before. Our poor Isabella was a good deal agitated at my leaving her, but was doing well, when unfortunately the Doctor advised her to try & walk across the room. She did so, and was in consequence attacked with severest pain – not neuralgic – and has since been obliged to take a great deal of opium. She is again better, and is struggling for strength enough to join me in Canada this winter. I doubt much whether she will be able to muster vigour enough to do so, and I fear that neither Margaret nor Louisa will be able to go to New York to look after matters.

Poor Mamma has again been attacked with another apoplectic affection, and only the most prompt and vigorous measures have restored her. She is still very weak and prostrate, but the present fit has passed away. The medical men say however, that she is not safe from another attack a single moment, and that the slightest indiscretion in diet, or the least disorder of stomach might cause a recurrence. Under these circumstances Marg^t must stay at home & poor Louisa requires nursing herself. So you see we are in a nice mess. I can only hope that Isa may rally so as to be able to travel homewards. If not I must look for some respectable person as a sort of companion for her during the winter. The *Boy* is flourishing like a *Green bay Horse* so writes Margaret, and that he is becoming strong & fat. Poor Maria has been suffering from inflammation since her return but is now better. I just heard an incident from a friend of mine here. His father in law is now in Scotland & happened to be at Loch Laggan when the Queen was there. He was standing amidst a crowd of Highlanders who were waiting to see their Sovereign, and who had after the fashion of their country & in her honour, all uncovered the *antipodes* of their heads, when his attention was attracted by an intelligent lad dressed, or undressed, in full Highland costume. They entered into conversation & the lad finding my friend was a Canadian asked him if he knew his two Aunts Isabella & Maria that lived in Canada. It was an odd rencontre was it not? The lad must have either been Andrew or Alexander Nuide.[25] We have no news here at all and I feel quite solitary & miserable living in lodgings alone. I would spend a pleasant winter, if Isabella were only here, as I have just enough work to keep me from *ennui*, and not so much as to absorb my attention.

I hope & trust Jane continues better. Give my love to her & believe me as ever my dearest sister,

yours affectionately,
John A. Macdonald

Isa's letters are up to the 24th

20 ISABELLA MACDONALD TO MARGARET GREENE

[Kingston, 1848]

My own most precious & most darling Sister,

I sincerely sympathize in your leaving dear, dear Mrs Biddle & most precious Husband. Full well I know how your spirit *must* be borne down by the hourly *yearning* for her society. For that unfailing *true-hearted* friendship and communion – earth alas! so *very* seldom affords. My dear, *dear* Mrs Biddle, how I *reverence* her worth, her *true-heartedness*, her *never* to-be-doubted *truth* of feeling *under all* circumstances. My darling sister it is perfectly holy, & my very soul bows before her as one God's Holy Spirit has given us for an example, but to which alas! alas! I may not hope to attain. My dear, dear Mrs Biddle. How I reverence her! How my weary *weary* spirit bows before her. May God's holiest, richest mercies *rest, now & ever, abidingly* on her and hers.

---

[25]Actually Macpherson of Nuide. Nuide is a small estate in Badenoch. Andrew and Alexander were probably the children of Ann Clark, who married a Macpherson.

I have only now got your letter darling sister saying you were to be in New York on 3rd & as you *felt* obliged to leave so idolized a friend, I rejoice you are with Mrs Field. Dear beautiful, *Porcelain* Mrs Field.[26] so different from the *gilt delf* of every day life. I really would dread seeing her often, my own darling precious sister, *you* know how *headlong* I ever go & I much fear I would love her but too fondly. Most strange how her presence carries me back to years I was not with you, & when gazing in her face I *live* in them. I really *yearn to look* on her again, to hear *her voice* & look at those beautiful eyes. To me her bright, *sparkling* society would be a rich blessing, & to the last I hoped to see her at Swampscott[27] last year. You will smile darling sister, at this relic of other days – in my feeling thus. But *you* know *what* she is, & her beautiful love for you makes her sacred to me. I *so long* to see her sit beside my bed again & her beautiful daughter sitting on it. I really now wonder how I ever had the courage – the *self-denial* – to obey the doctors in New York, and sometimes refuse her. I know they need not ask it now. But I must finish darling sister. It is very late and John is receiving company downstairs, & Baby is asleep beside me. He is not well & oh darling darling sister my very soul is bound up in him. God pardon me if I sin in this. But did I not purchase him dearly?

All are as usual – only 3 clergymen have been attacked shamefully in the street here. Dont mention it as John might not like *my* telling it you. Maria and her girls are nicely. Baby's cold is I hope better – it will be better shortly I hope. God in Heaven bless and watch over you my darling sister. Love to *all* friends now around you. Oh! our poor *poor* Uncle! how I dread your seeing him.[28] Oh! that his sufferings were in mercy ended! Tell me please how you are *really* & ever believe in my sleepless love and gratitude. What can I take from *this* for you darling darling sister? Do tell me at once.

[26]Unidentified.
[27]Swampscott, Massachusetts, near Boston.
[28]It seems most likely that the uncle was a Clark since all the possible Shaw uncles were dead by this time, but as none of the names of Alexander Clark's brothers (or sisters) are known there is no way of being sure. Can Margaret Greene have been sailing to Scotland from New York? Or was the uncle in America?

My dearest Sister–   *Kingston, July 9, 1848*

Next Tuesday Isabella will have been at home for a fortnight. She bore the journey wonderfully well, the desire to see her child keeping her up, & not in any prejudiced [*sic*] by the fatigue with the exception of a cold which she caught on the way. For some time after her arrival and after the excitement was over, there was a considerable reaction, and she was much exhausted. Her cough too shook her grievously, but some prescription given her by Doctor Hayward has relieved her, and she is now nearly free of it.

She daily continues her exertions to sit up a little and contrives to do so for about ten minutes. Yesterday she suffered from pain, and was obliged to have recourse to opium, and to day she complains of the lassitude and discomforts consequent on taking it. If she is fortunate enough to get a comfortable night's rest, I trust she will be able to resume her attempts to take exercise tomorrow. She has now, one source of interest which was denied her, the society of her boy. At first he was shy & uncomfortable in her room, which is in some degree darkened and as she could not dandle him, or toss him about, a ceremony which the young gentleman insists upon from all who approach him. He is now however great friends with her, and sits most contentedly in the bed with her surrounded by his toys, which he throws about, much to her inconvenience I am sure, tho' she will not allow it. He is very healthy, and observant & altogether an interesting child and poor Isa, as well as your humble servant, are as you may suppose very proud of him. As for Mamma, I really believe she dreams of him all night, certain it is that she talks of him all day.

Isabella had your letter of the [29] today. The only one which she has received since she came home. She is distressed to learn that poor dear Jane has been so ill again. Your next note, will we trust bring better news. She has had at the same time a letter from Maria. All her young ones are well and much improved by the seabathing, altho' the weather has been wet and unpropitious. Mrs. Lowther's little party have also benefited by the change. I have not written to or heard from you for a long time dear sister, but now that Isabella is once more at home with me I will send you a due allowance of bulletins, until she is able to play scribe for

[29]Left blank.

herself. All our household are well, as are the Harpers. Give my love to Jane, and believe me my dear sister,

your most affectionately
John A. Macdonald

22 TO MARGARET GREENE

Kingston August 1, 1848

Another week has passed, my dearest sister, without letters from you. Isabella feels uneasy and would be more so, did she not know the irregularities and delays of the American Post Office Department. We are in daily expectation of a letter. Isabella has not varied in her state of health since I wrote last. She is still weak, and suffers occasionally and severely from neuralgia. This is nothing but the old story, and therefore does not make one so uneasy as the tenderness and sensitiveness of her lungs, which the slightest cold affects.

Before she left New York, she was troubled with an occasional pain in her chest, and slight cough. She brought it with her, and I suppose increased it on the way, for the first week after she was at home she coughed incessantly. She threw it off however, but still the hacking cough returns, and makes me very anxious. On her route & after her arrival, there were occasional appearances of blood from her lungs, but both Doctors Johnston & Hayward told her such would be the case in consequence of the fatigues and excitement of her journey. I spoke to Hayward two days ago about the cough. He says it arises from the tenderness of the lungs, but that he discerns no symptoms of ulceration or permanent affection – but I fear, I fear. I hope my next will give you better tidings. Do not mistake me, however, she is not worse than when I wrote last, but the continuance of the cough alarms me.

All the rest of our household are well. Master John who is looking forward to his birthday tomorrow is in high spirits and in capital condition. Certainly there never was a child who has got through his first year with less trouble or illness of any kind. God grant it may continue so. We have not heard lately of or from Maria. She will I fancy, soon be wending homewards.

Pray give all manner of love from Isa & myself to Jane & believe me as ever my dearest sister,

yours most affectionately
John A. Macdonald

23 To Margaret Greene

Kingston August 15, 1848

I was rather out of sorts last week, my dearest sister, with a suspicion of intermittent,[30] but I soon threw it off and am now all right again. I did not write, but Isa sent you a scrap last week, and now I resume the duty of reporting progress. Isabella continues as before, not suffering so much from tic but still more than enough to make her very uncomfortable. The chills which she complains of are lighter during the last week, and will I trust soon disappear. The chief cause of uneasiness is the occasional appearance of blood in her handkerchief when she coughs.

On the whole, I think her a good deal better than at the time of the last bulletin. I have taken a cottage or rather, I beg its pardon a *Villa*[31] near Harper's cottage to which we remove, Isa, the baby and I, on Saturday. It is a large roomy house where I hope to see you and Jane next spring. The house was build for a retired grocer, who was resolved to have a "Eyetalian Willar", and has built the most fantastic concern imaginable. From the previous laudable tho' rather prosaic pursuits of the worthy landlord the house is variously known in Kingston as Tea Caddy Castle, Molasses Hall & Muscovado Cottage.

As it is not respectable either for a man or a house to have an alias we must fix on some one name and I leave it to Jane's good taste to select out of the above, the most appropriate name for our habitat.

John the younger flourisheth mightily as do all other friends. With love to Jane believe me as ever, my dearest Sister,

yours affectionately
John A. Macdonald

P.S. A *propos* of my landlord – here is a conundrum for Jane. Why is mixing wine or adulterating sugar a more heinous crime than murder? ANS. Because murder is a gross offence but adulterating sugar is a *grocer offence.*

24 To Margaret Greene

Kingston August 29, 1848

I made our final move to our new habitation, on Friday evening last, my dearest sister, and we are now trying to make ourselves comfortable in

[30]Intermittent fever.
[31]Bellevue House, now a Macdonald museum.

Pekoe Pagoda as we call it, until Jane gives us a better name. Isabella suffered a great deal from the journey, which though less than a mile exhausted her much. Fortunately Dr Hayward was here, and accompanied us on the way. After four days' rest, she now begins to feel the advantage of the complete quiet and seclusion of the house, which is completely surrounded with trees, and has a fresh breeze ever blowing on it from Lake Ontario. I regret to say that Isa suffers tic without much if any cessation, and is obliged to take opium daily. I still am sanguine as to the effect of a week's quiet on her system.

I have had a long and serious conversation respecting Isa's health a day or two ago, with Dr Hayward, the gentleman, you may remember, who accompanied her from New York, and who when there conferred with Dr Johnston as to his treatment. Dr Johnston was of opinion that her left lung was affected, but to what extent he could not say. She has a slight cough, and occasional exhibitions (in small quantities) of blood on her handkerchief, from her lungs. Hayward says that these symptoms, the cough & the blood of course indicate something wrong, some cause of irritation. And yet she has none of the evidences on which a medical man could state there was any ulceration. There is no appearance of pus, or of any other matter, when she coughs. Her pulse is not feverish or accelerated, and she has never shown a hectic spot on her cheek. The Doctors agree that all that can be done is to use the necessary means to stop the hemorrage when it comes and to soothe the cough when troublesome, and that nature must do the rest. Thus stands the case at present. She is in God's hands and we must abide the result.

The nurse and child came out with us, & he is in good health.[32] He sits by the hour now with his Mother, as contentedly as possible, and smiles & crows away from one end of the day to the other. He will be weaned in about a fortnight or three weeks, as the weather becomes cooler. You mention in one of your letters that you want to know how to secure Ann's[33] legacy if it is ever procured. Let it be invested in some security in the name of two trustees for her benefit. Her husband's creditors will have no means of getting at it, or indeed of knowing anything about it. Isa bids me tell you with her love that she has got your

---

[32]Little John Alexander Macdonald died suddenly, three weeks later, of unknown causes.
[33]Margaret Greene and Isabella Macdonald had a sister Ann, married to a Captain Macpherson, who lived in New Zealand.

59

shawls which she will send to New York by the first opportunity. Tell Jane we were much puzzled by her enigmatical seal which was somewhat of this kind I 2 BU, and that I read it thus— I *long* to be with you. Is that correct? With sincere love to Jane & yourself I am as always my dearest sister,

most affectionately yours
John A. Macdonald

25 TO MARGARET GREENE

Kingston December 3, 1848

I returned last week from Toronto, my dearest sister, where I had been for the fortnight previous, attending the sittings of the Court of Queen's Bench. I left poor dear Isabella in her usual state, suffering occasionally from pain, and only able to move from the bed to the sofa, but still patient resigned and uncomplaining as ever. On my return I found her stronger and better. She had been practising sitting up for a few minutes daily in my absence, in order to be able to surprise me by coming to dinner which she effected. We had our little table brought to her bed room, and there we dined in State. For the last three days she has not been so well. The tic has been troubling her much and yesterday she had it severely in her head and has been obliged to take large doses of opium. To day she says she is better though weak, languid and miserable from the effects of the medicine. I am in hopes that the attack is over and that tomorrow or next day she will be able to resume her habits of exercise. Her time passes very monotonously out here but not, I think unpleasantly. I leave the house every morning about nine oclock, and she is there alone, unless when occasionally visited by one of the family or Dr Hayward, when he is in town. But her time does not hang heavily on her hands. She has as much to do as she is able for, in directing the household affairs managing her servants &c, and I can assure you, such is her attention and method that confined to the room though she be, she makes a capital housekeeper. Every thing is nice and tidy about the house, and *my* dinner, the great event of each day, about which poor Isa takes the greatest pains, is served up as well as one would wish it. And all this too, with the most laudable attention to economy, & horror of waste. I usually return home about six in the evening, and after dinner I read to her, while she knits &c till tea time, and so passes the day. I am much disappointed at your not receiving my letters. I make it a point to write every Sunday, or Monday morning in time for the mail of that day, and my letters are always mailed by one of my clerks. So that the fault must lie in the American Post Office. Maria is better & in good spirits. She is talking of buying a cottage in Kingston. Her throat does not trouble her so much as formerly. Dr Hayward says it is not regular bronchitis but a chronic relaxation of the throat. Her children are well. My mother & sisters are well, as is Mrs Lowther & her family. Henry McPherson won a scholarship at Queen's College the other day though only a freshman but little Lowther's health is very precarious.[34] Rae of Hamilton has failed in business once again and poor Helen Macpherson is again at the foot of the ladder.[35] With sincere love to Jane we unite in sending you our warmest wishes & affection.

Ever yours, sincerely
John A. Macdonald

Please return the enclosed.

26 To Margaret Greene

Kingston Dec. 17, 1848

I allowed Isabella to write for herself last Sunday, my dearest sister and it is now my turn. The poor girl has had two days suffering of neuralgia in the head, but is now better again, and for the last three days has allowed me to draw her into dinner in a chair. This fatigues her a little, but still it is better she should have some exercise. Could she but regain some strength I would hope for her recovery, but she is very, very weak. Her mind is composed and tranquil, almost cheerful, and her time is fully taken up with household affairs and looking after my comfort, I shall be obliged to go down to Montreal at the end of next month, but not for long. The idea of my going however distresses her so much that I

[34]Henry and Lowther Pennington Macpherson, Jr., were the older and younger sons of the late Lowther Pennington Macpherson. Henry became a lawyer and practised at Owen Sound, Ontario. In 1865, Macdonald, as Attorney General, surrendered to a barrage of urgent letters from Henry Macpherson, and made him County Court Judge of Grey County.
[35]Thomas Rae was a Hamilton merchant and sometime shipowner.

would not go, were it not a matter of necessity. She is just putting the finishing stitch to a new waistcoat for me, which I am to sport as a winter vest. Isa, has, thank God but little cough just now, & that appears caused by weakness & relaxation of the system and not from any pulmonary disease. She sends all kinds of love to you & Jane. Maria is again suffering with her throat which is ulcerated again. She is the most heedless and imprudent person in the world, going out into the open air without bonnet or shawl and in all weathers. Her children are I believe all well. I saw Jenny yesterday as big and burly as possible.

We have no winter yet, the weather is pleasant and warm, No snow, and but little rain. This is unusual and we don't like it, but I really think we have been warmer than you have been at Athens. All are well at my mother's house, at Harpers and Mrs Lowthers. Kiss Jane for me & believe me as ever,

your affectionate brother
John A. Macdonald

27 To Margaret Greene

My dearest Sister   Kingston July 24, 1849
We had the pleasure of your brother John's society for about three weeks. He left us on Friday to visit Sir Hew Dalrymple[36] for a day or two & then off to Philadelphia. He was very much worried at the idea of being on this side of the Atlantic without seeing you, but there was no remede. Poor Isabella enjoyed his society so much, he was so considerate & judicious in his visits to her that she was not at all overtasked or fatigued by it. But his presence of course brought Maria & other friends about us, and Isa thought it necessary to see them. This has been too much for her altogether and fatigue added to the agitation of parting made her quite ill. She has had a severe, nay an alarming attack of dysentery (not a mere diarrhoea) which has again reduced her to the very lowest state of prostration. I really thought on Sunday that she would not be able to rally. She is now, thank God, on the mend again. The dysentery has ceased &

[36]Sir Hew Hamilton Dalrymple, Bart., was lieutenant-colonel of the 71st Highland Regiment, then stationed at St. Jean. John Clark was married to Sir Hew Dalrymple's sister, Charlotte Sophia Dalrymple. At least three of John Clark's children were given the second name Dalrymple.

she is comparatively easy but unable to raise her hand to her head. The whole gain of this spring is gone & we have not more than two months & a half of summer left.

The cholera is raging greatly in several sections of the Province & through the neighboring States. It is not so severe here, as in most other places. In fact no persons but those of dissipated habits have died of it here. Still every body feels & suffers from the premonitory symptoms of cholera. Your brother so much that I made him see a medical man. He was kept in the house & on the sofa for 5 or 6 days. He left here however, I am happy to say restored. Poor Maria is just now suffering severely from the same cause, to such a degree as to be confined to bed. The rest of our friends are all well. We have just now a Convention of the British party about to meet in Kingston.[37] Their sittings take place tomorrow and attract a great deal of attention in this part of the world.

It will I think put its foot on the idea of annexation. I am delighted to learn so frequently of dear little Jenny's continued progress. Are there any beaux in your part of the world? Who has she got to tease? By the way your brother has taken a fancy to our climate & says he will try for a staff appointment here. They are rather scarce however & it may be many years before a suitable vacancy offers. I took him up the Bay of Quinté and showed him so fine farms, beautiful scenery & bad roads. He was much struck with the lake on the mountain forty miles above Kingston, and compared to Loch-an-Eilean, near Dalnavert. Good bye my dear sister— with bushels of love for Jane, I am as ever,

yours most affectionately
John A. Macdonald

28 To Margaret Greene

My dearest Sister   Kingston Dec. 9, 1849
During the last week, Isabella has been struggling with her feelings— Her duty to others especially to her unborn offspring[38] compelled

---

[37]The British American League was an association formed in Montreal in April 1849, whose purpose was to find remedies for "the commercial and industrial depression" and for the "evils of a social and political character" of the day. It was a theoretically non-partisan, but actually thoroughly Conservative, body. The convention, of which Macdonald was a principal organizer, was held at Kingston, July 25-31, 1849, and recommended tariff protection to native industry, a reduction in official salaries, and the confederation of the British North American provinces.
[38]The future Hugh John Macdonald.

her to subdue all agitation, & she was apparently calm & resigned for most of the time, but the struggle has been too much for her. Her anguish of mind banished sleep, and this brought on exhaustion, bleeding from the throat, and a terrible attack of neuralgia. Last night she was fearfully ill, so ill that I was much alarmed about her. To day she lies in a state of complete exhaustion, but her sufferings are not so severe. I attribute this attack altogether to the attempted suppression of her emotions, but now that sorrow has had its way, I trust she will not to night have a recurrence of her sufferings.

You are right in supposing that her thoughts are constantly dwelling on your bereavement,[39] on your sufferings. She sorrows more for you than for Jane, & continually asks the question, "What will become of poor sister now, it will break her heart". I do my best to console her, and have already interested her in a thousand little schemes about having you here. Schemes which I sincerely hope you will enable us to realize. You seem to think that you cannot leave Athens before spring. I trust that then at all events we will see you.

Should you come to the determination of leaving at once the place where you have suffered so much & of coming north, you would not suffer much fatigue in coming here. From New York to New Haven by steam, & from New Haven by Albany to Rome by railway will bring you within 50 miles of Kingston & those 50 miles can easily be travelled if our winter roads are formed. However I will not yet press you to take any course. Your loss is too recent and constantly in your thoughts to justify me in doing so. Isabella thinks with me that you are not at all equal to the task of bringing up your poor brothers orphans.[40] Such a charge would be one of unmixed trouble & annoyance to you, without a corresponding benefit to them. Their habits, manners and way of thinking are now in a great measure formed, and you would be constantly wounded & distressed by their conduct & habits, which will be too confirmed to be amended. Were they so young as to be capable of training as you would wish them, the charge tho' a heavy one, would bring its reward but I fear that it is now too late.

Isa says that if our darling Jane had had the selection of the memorial to mark where her remains were to rest, she would have chosen a simple & unadorned stone, and she says that she knows well that your

[39]The death of Jane Clark, November 13, 1849, at the age of thirty-seven.
[40]The same orphans, presumably, that Isabella referred to in her letter of June 11, 1845. There is nothing to indicate that they were ever cared for by Mrs. Greene.

own choice will be in correspondence with Jane's retiring, & unostentatious character. She would much like to have the drawing & inscription as settled upon by you.

From her heart she thanks you for the ring. But she cannot bear the idea of your scattering the ornaments & clothing of her departed sister. You have associations connected with them that no one else can have. You will have a melancholy pleasure in having them near you while in some quarters they would be thought of only with reference to their money value. As to the clothing the parting with every article that you had seen her wear would give you a separate pang and this would not be compensated by the reflection that they were divided among a number of children. She hopes you will retain them yourself and for yourself & not needlessly inflict a wound on your most sacred feelings. Isa views her coming trials with great fortitude & from her courage & patience I have every hope of a happy issue. Still she prepare for the worst. She has now the portraits of both her sisters whom she loved so well[41] opposite her bed. Last night she told me, to send you, should things go ill with her, the portrait of your departed one, and this I promised to do. It is not impossible that she may be confined next month. Dr Hayward or Mair or perhaps both will attend her.

I think you had better retain the desk &c until spring when you come north. At this season of the year there is little communication if any between New York & Canada & the parcel would run great risk of being mislaid. I now write— 10 PM at Isa's bedside. She has just taken an opiate & is lying quiet. I trust that she will ere long fall asleep & escape the fearful agonies of last night. Ever my dear sister,

your most affectionate brother
John A. Macdonald

29 To Margaret Greene

Kingston Dec. 12, 1849

Since I wrote last, my dearest sister, Isabella has been very ill and prostrate. Things, I am happy to say are on the mend again, and she is much easier & stronger today. Her bed had not been made for ten days,

---

[41]This may refer to another sister, whose name is unknown, who had died at some earlier date.

but this evening I managed to have her shifted to the sofa & she has now got back, much fatigued with the change, but is now, of course more comfortable. We are looking out anxiously for letters from you. Isa is much afraid that the reaction, the want of employment for your energies, so long overtasked, will have a prejudicial effect on your health.

I trust you have thrown off the fever hanging about you. You have mental griefs enough, without being subjected to the distressing depression arising from fever & weakness. All our friends here are well. Maria & her children doing very nicely. My mother is very strong this winter, but has had one or two bad attacks.

She is perfectly aware of the perilous nature of these attacks and is perfectly resigned to her probable fate and sudden exit. My sister Margaret is wintering at Quebec with Mrs Wilson. I trust to hear by tomorrow's post of your returning strength & spirits. Believe me my dear sister,

always yr affectionate brother
John A. Macdonald

30 To Margaret Greene

My dear Sister   Kingston Jan. 6, 1850

Isabella has been in great pain for some three or four days, but I am happy to say, she is better tonight and in less pain. Her sufferings are not from tic, but from her situation. She was in the same way in New York, and they betoken an approaching *accouchement*. I am glad to say that she is not all nervous at the anticipation, and seems to have no anxiety or apprehensions as to the result. All arrangements have been long made, and she now waits for the issue with patience and fortitude. She has given me many directions about herself and her offspring, which any evil happen, & having done all that she can do, is now content. It is her wish, as it is mine, that in case the child should be girl, you should name it. Should it be a male, Isabella says she will accept it as the return of her firstborn and will give it the same name.

We hope to receive the expression of your wishes in this matter, my dear sister in answer to this, as the infant may be an independent existence before this reaches you. Dr Mair a person whom Isa likes much attends her. He is on the medical staff here and is one of the best of men. As he has not made midwifery a matter of practice with him, he will act as consulting physician, and his present intention is to call in Dʳ Dickson, a person in whom he expresses great confidence and who is a very respectable medical practitioner here. A very nice woman, a Mrs Sutherland, has been retained as nurse, and so we are all prepared. Isa is in God's hands and there we must leave her.

You must be much worn down and debilitated my dearest sister by continual attacks of chill & fever. Had you not better leave Athens and try Savannah.

We say here in the north that a change of air, even to a worse atmosphere drives away fever. Nothing is so harassing to body & mind, so depressing to the spirits as a lingering slow fever and it would be well for you to throw it off by a change of scene.

Maria & her children are well as are my mother & sisters. Isa & I unite in our sincerest love & esteem for you. You must pardon my not writing a more connected note but it is late & I have just finished a long letter to your brother John. Poor fellow, he will now feel more than ever the unhappy chance which prevented his visit to you last summer. Good night my dearest sister. I will add a note tomorrow morning as to how Isa is then.

Always yours affectionately
John A. Macdonald

Monday

Isa had a better night than usual, but is now in a good deal of pain. I would not be surprised if her illness came on within this week or the next.

JAMᶜD

31 TO MARGARET GREENE

[Kingston] Jan. 20, [1850]
We are delighted to learn, my dear sister, from your letter of the 12ᵗʰ that your fever & chills have left you for a season. I trust the departure will be permanent, and that fever has gone to return no more. We are here as when I last wrote, for the last two days Isabella has been rather easier and more free from pain than usual, but she is not so strong as I

67

would wish her under her present circumstances. Still she keeps her courage up and is as resolute and free from nervousness as you could desire. Our weather is as fine as weather can be. I wish you were here to enjoy it, clear, sunny & cool, not *cold* – that is to say not *too* cold. Not unpleasant to walk and still receiving comfort from the sight of the fire. My mother walked thro' the snow from her house to ours today after church and spent the afternoon with Isa. She is wonderfully strong this winter and yet I doubt not that you will see a sad falling off even from the time when you saw her last. All our friends here are well and flourishing. I have to day written a long letter to Anne[42] which she will see about six months hence. What changes may occur in the meantime! Perhaps the writer, perhaps those he most loves may be removed before the letter reaches its destination – and perhaps when it arrives, there may be no one on earth to receive it. I believe otherwise, I have a strong feeling that our circle will not soon again be narrowed. The rod cannot be always smiting.

Since September last I have been alone & without a partner. Isa says I work too hard, & in truth I begin to feel that I do, but like a thief on the treadmill, I *must* step on, or be dragged. I am now deep in the mysteries of hydropathy sitz-douche, & friction are the order of the day, & if I forget my *quantum* of tumblers of *aqua pura*, Isabella is pulling my ears at once.[43] Poor soul, you will wonder to see her management of household affairs from her bed. She is like the "Invisible Lady" that used to exhibit not "show" herself some years ago. The invisible Lady's voice, orders & behests are heard & obeyed all over the house, & are carried out as to cupboards which she never sees & pots & pans that have no acquaintance with her. Not a glass is broken or set of dishes diminished, but she knows of, and calls the criminal to account for. In fact she carries on the whole machinery, as well, to appearance as if she were bustling from *but* to *ben* in person. Good night my dearest sister. Isa joins in love with yrs affectionately

J. A. Macdonald

---

[42]Ann Macpherson, living in New Zealand.
[43]It is not clear whether Macdonald or Isabella was being treated by hydropathy— a cure involving the internal and external application of water. A sitz-douche was a hip bath.

Kingston Jan. 27, 1850

I received your letter, my dearest sister containing the drawing, which I have given to Isa. She keeps it constantly beside her, & often refers to it. Isa is still dragging on a daily existence of pain & suffering which she bears with her usual quiet resignation. There are no greater signs of approaching illness than when I wrote last, but Dr Mair thinks it just about to come on. Her nurse sleeps in the next room to her, and every thing is prepared, but she may linger on, as at New York for weeks in suffering.

This is much to be dreaded as she is weaker than when at New York, and this continual agony wears her down. She is delighted at the improvement in your health, and is looking forward with pleasurable anticipation to your meeting in the spring.

It will be a sad enough meeting, & yet will bring a melancholy satisfaction with it.

I am truly sorry to learn from your letter that Mr Robinson is so much afflicted. I have a very grateful recollection of his kindness and attention to me at Philadelphia when there with Isa some years ago. I sincerely trust his health will be reestablished. All our friends here are well. Maria is getting absolutely fat & round. She is kind and attentive to Isa. I have written to New York about the box meant for you. It was taken from here by a Kingston merchant, who left it at a shipping office somewhere there. I would not be at all surprised, if it were found lying in the warehouse, where it was left. Mr Harper has gone to N.Y. on business and will probably before his return go all the way to Natchez. It is not likely that he will come near you in his travels.

We are all quiet politically in this country. The annexation cry meets with very little encouragement and if England only behaves decently to us, she may retain these colonies for any length of time. I wish you were in Kingston just now. I have never seen such delightful weather. Not too cold & yet bracing & healthy. If the latter half is as fine as the former has been, we will indeed be fortunate. Good night my dearest sister. I trust this will find you completely restored to physical health & strength. Time can alone cure the mental wound, which has caused you so much anguish. Always my dear Sister,

yours affectionately
John A. Macdonald

33 TO MARGARET GREENE

My dearest Sister   *Kingston Feb.* 2, *1850*

There is no change in Isabella's situation as yet. She still lingers on and suffers and submits. I am glad to say that yesterday and today she has been a little easier & is considerably stronger. You would be surprised and gratified at seeing her calm courage. She contemplates her approaching sufferings with the greatest possible resolution and cheerfulness, and better than all, she has no fears or despondency as to the result.

How long she may remain in this state, I cannot say nor can the medical men. They look for a change every hour. Isa sends you a thousand loves, and bids me say to you that you must knit her a pair of infant socks and send or rather bring them north. All our friends here are well. Poor Margaret has been ill at Quebec at Ann Wilson's but is now better. It is late at night, and I shall not send this off till Monday. So I will be able to report tomorrow & next day to you. Good Night.
Sunday.

Isabella had a tolerable night & is now comparatively easy. Still no more indications of a change than there have been for three weeks.
Monday.

Isa is very weak and miserable this morning. She had a night of great discomfort & pain. Her immediate confinement is much to be desired, this continuance of suffering wears down her strength and renders her less able to bear the approaching illness.

I have written to New York ab^t the box which has been mislaid in some extraordinary manner & hope to find it. In great haste alwys my dearest Sister,

yours with affection
John A. Macdonald

34 TO MARGARET GREENE

My dearest Sister   [*Kingston*] Feb. 18, [1850]

Isa has been suffering greatly, so much so, that Dr Mair was of opinion that her time had come and she therefore continued to suffer on without taking any of the soothing powders for many hours. At last the Doctor has allowed her to take them again, & she has had some relief.

The struggle has exhausted her very much, but she has kept up her spirits and longs for the time when her anxieties & agonies will cease. I do not apprehend nor do the medical men, any danger for her, but still it is terrible to see her struggle & suffer as she does.

Tuesday.
     Isa had a good night last night & this morning is strong & in good spirits. She anxiously prays for her trouble to come on today. I shall write you again tomorrow.

Yours ever
John A. Macdonald

35 TO MARGARET MACDONALD

My dear Margaret   *Kingston April 2, 1850*
     I received your kind and considerate letter of congratulation. We have got Johnnie back again almost his image.[44] I don't think he is so pretty, but he is not so delicate. He was born fat & coarse. Isa was very anxious that he should get his *own* name again for she considers him almost the same being, but I think it right that the feelings of those we esteem should not be outraged by doing so. Mamma, Maria, Mrs Greene & many others have a prejudice against the renaming a child. What his name may be therefore we will leave to be settled until you come up. Mrs. Greene & you will arrive about the same time & I will leave it to the female conclave.
     I need not say that your presence is anxiously looked for. Mamma had one of her attacks on Friday, (Good Friday) and it still hangs about her to an unsafe extent. She seems lethargic, & not so free of speech as before, but I trust the active treatment she is under may set her up again. Meanwhile it is well to be always prepared for the worst news, and if any thing went wrong I would not hesitate to advise you of it at once by telegraph.

[44]Hugh John Macdonald was born March 13, 1850.

My poor friend Charles Stuart is very low.[45] How long he may live I know not. His fate is decided. He *may* live until autumn. He *may* die tomorrow. For my part I fear the worst. When I go to bed at night, I fear to hear of his death in the morning. He refuses to take all advice & all medicine except from myself, & I get thoroughly scolded & abused for the peremptory manner in which I play the Doctor. I trust the Wilsons are in some degree calmed down, & able to bear the recollection of their loss. I can sympathize with them fully. They lost their last child, I lost my only one, and when I did lose him I never expected another. This is a sad enough letter, but these kinds of letters become common as people get older. Tho' yet a young man many, very many of my companions have disappeared and my firmest & best friend is about to leave me.

Isa, who is not at all well and who lingers very much in her recovery joins me in love to you. Always my dear Marg^t,

your affectionate brother
John A. Macdonald

I have used mourning paper since poor Jane's death. Lest it might frighten you I have written all well round the *seal*.

36 To Louisa Macdonald

My dear Louisa   *Quebec Oct. 13, 1852*

I have received your two letters, and I must apologize for not answering the first sooner.

I had no particular reason for not doing so, except that I was very busy and did not anticipate there was any hurry about it.

Mr Williamson first told me of it, but I had no intimation from him that there was an intention to hurry the marriage.[46] In fact I learnt noth-

[45]Charles Stuart was a member of a distinguished Canadian family, the most prominent of which were his three uncles, Archdeacon George Okill Stuart of Kingston, Sir James Stuart, Chief Justice of the Court of Queen's Bench of Lower Canada, and Hon. Andrew Stuart, Solicitor General of Lower Canada, 1838-40. Charles Stuart's father, also named Charles, was for a time Sheriff of the Midland District of Upper Canada, and the younger Charles was Recorder of Frontenac County, 1840-50. Charles Stuart was probably Macdonald's closest friend until his death, a few days after this letter was written, on April 7, 1850.

[46]Margaret Macdonald and Professor Williamson were married on October 19, 1852, but John A. Macdonald was not, in the end, able to attend.

ing more from him than the fact of the engagement, with which I expressed my satisfaction.

I said that I thought a careful person, some respectable widow, more a companion than a mere servant should be engaged to act as a an [sic] attendant for Mamma. I have no idea of imposing her on Mr Williamson, and depend upon it, it is better that she should remain in her own house. Margaret won't live far from her, and can see her every day.

I shall strain every nerve to be up on the 19th but I am a member of the General Election Committee & have taken an oath to attend regularly. At present I know nothing to prevent my going up, & there is no present probability of my being detained but a [sic] something might arise to keep me nailed to my post & so I give you notice of it for fear of disappointment. My intention is, if nothing prevents, to leave here on Saturday night next.

I wish that Moll should have a good kit, & I wish you to expend £25, for her in such things as you like. Don't say anything to her about it, but when I go up I will settle the bills. Get the things.

Give my love to Mamma & take it for yourself. I drop a line to Moll.

Yours affectionately
John A. Macdonald

37 To Louisa Macdonald

My dear Louisa   Quebec Feb. 21, 1855

I have been overwhelmed with work in getting ready for Parliament, which will account for your not hearing from me before. I am, thank God, in good health and spirits & quite ready for the Parliamentary campaign. I like Sir Edmund[47] very much he is a thorough man of business, & attends to the public interests *Con amore*. I am glad to hear such good accounts from Mamma. Give her my love & say I will be up as soon as Parliament rises. Isa has been too ill to write. You should see her oftener & write me.

It is impossible for me to tell, what the Parl' may do ab' the seat of Gov' until they meet. I think however, my house will be vacated, & it is

---

[47]Sir Edmund Head, Governor of the Province of Canada, 1854-61.

quite at the service of Mamma & the rest of you.[48] I enclose a *memo* for Mr Williamson. Love to all. In haste,

Yrs ever
John A. Macdonald

Let Henry Macpherson write me in full before he settles down. I may be able to give him a lift.

38 To Louisa Macdonald

My dear Louisa   *Quebec Sept. 21, 1855*

I have just rec'd your letter. I have no decided plans as yet. So must ask you to continue in your present house or get another one, as if there was no chance of getting into mine.

Even if it is finally decided that Isabella is to go to Toronto, I have been unable to go there to make arrangements for her reception so that it will be the middle of October before she can be moved.

If you possibly could get Mrs Chambers to give you the house to 1st May it would suit all parties.

But by no means part with the Williamsons.[49] I don't mind the expense of a year's rent. Say nothing to Isabella on the subject, of any kind or nature whatsoever.

Give my love to Mamma & tell her I hope to see her by the first week in October. I will go up with the Gov.ᵗ & return perhaps to Quebec. love to Margᵗ & her husband.

Yours affectionately
John A. Macdonald

---

[48]The provincial government was moved from Quebec to Toronto in October 1855. Isabella and Hugh also moved to Toronto from Kingston.
[49]From shortly after Margaret's marriage until this time Mrs. Macdonald and Louisa lived with the Williamsons. When Isabella and Hugh were moved to Toronto, the Williamsons moved into Macdonald's house on Brock Street (which burned down in 1856). Mrs. Macdonald and Louisa lived by themselves until 1860, in houses on Collingwood Street and on Johnson Street.

39 To James Williamson

My dear Sir   *Quebec Sept. 29, 1855*

   It will be impossible to get you a set of Journals[50] &c until after we are settled in Toronto. I shall attend to it then. There is I believe a stock of old Journals on hand there, out of which a complete or nearly complete set may be gathered.

   I hope to see you all next week.

Yours vy faithfully
John A. Macdonald

40 To Mrs. Hugh Macdonald

My dearest Mother   *Toronto Jan. 26, 1856*

   Isabella has been very, very ill since I wrote last. She was so low one day that the Doctor sent for me to my office, thinking she was dying. She has rallied wonderfully again, and though still very weak and scarcely conscious, she is evidently on the mend. I sent Hugh every day to Mrs Cameron's to keep him out of the way and not to interfere with Janet[51] who was constantly employed in looking after Isabella. Hugh is very well and in good spirits. He is quite a favourite at the houses which he visits. They are Cameron's, Vankoughnet's, David Macpherson's and Lewis Moffatts.[52] At all these houses there are young people, well brought up so that he has the advantage of a good companionship. He and I play Beggar My Neighbour every evening and you can't fancy how delighted he is when he beats me. He knows the value of the cards as well as I do, and looks after his own interests sharply.

   I get lots of invitations here. I was asked out for every day last week, but declined of course, on account of Isa's illness. Next week or rather this week, it is the same thing. But I am obliged to refuse, as I am getting

---

[50]Journals of the Legislative Assembly, which the professor wanted for the Queen's library.

[51]Janet was a servant.

[52]Macdonald's close Toronto friends were a fairly substantial lot. Philip M. M. S. Vankoughnet was a successful lawyer (and later politician and judge), John Cameron was a banker, and David Lewis Macpherson was a wealthy business man and railway contractor. Lewis Moffat was a partner in a general merchandise company and a director of the Bank of British North America.

ready for Parliament. I trust my dear Mother, you are keeping well & that Moll is all right again. Pray give my love to her & Loo not forgetting the Professor. Believe me my dear Mother,

your affectionate son
John A. Macdonald

41 TO MRS. HUGH MACDONALD

My dearest Mother   Toronto Feb. 4, 1856

Isabella was desparately ill all last week, and was under treatment by Dr Telfer.

She is now better & I hope will in a few days be as usual. Hugh flourishes greatly. He is in very good health & spirits. Since Isa's illness he has spent his time principally at Rose Cameron's as Janet's time was taken up in attending to her. Sometimes he went to David Macpherson's and to Philip Vankoughnet's.

The weather here has been intensely cold, but I have not suffered much from it, as my house & office are close together. I am very busy in getting ready for Parliament.

It commences on the 15th and I will then have little rest night or day until the end of the Session. However I thrive wonderfully under it. Love to Marg^t Louisa & the Doctor. Always my dear Mother,

yr affectionate son
John A.

42 TO MRS. HUGH MACDONALD

My dearest Mother   Toronto March 17, 1856

I have been so much bothered lately about political matters that I have had but little time to write. We are all as usual however. Isabella has been tolerably well for some time and is in good spirits. Rose Cameron is a good deal with her and prevents her from being lonely.[53] For the last

---

[53]Almost forty years later Professor Williamson recalled that the Macdonald women "had opposed Isabella having so much to do with Mrs. Cameron". Why they did is not clear.

three days however she has suffered from the swelling of hands & feet which Dr Telfer says is erysipelas.

Hugh is, thank god, in prime health. He had a party of about sixteen, on his birthday & he has not got over his exertions or his stories of all their doings.

His teeth are coming out now without pain. He continually talks of Kingston however. Whenever he is asked whether he likes Kingston or Toronto best, he says always "I like Kingston best because my Grandmother lives there". I was a good deal out of sorts for a time but I am now all right & hard at work.

I am carrying on a war against that scoundrel George Brown and I will teach him a lesson that he never learnt before. I shall prove him a most dishonest, dishonorable fellow & in doing so I will only pay him a debt I owe him for abusing me for months together in his newspaper.[54]

Tell Mr Williamson that I have just seen Sir William Logan[55] who says he has got a book & map for him. I don't think the House will sit longer than the first of May. I shall then take a run down with Isabella & Hugh & pay you all a visit. Can you give us a bed?

We are now discussing the question of the seat of Government and an old Frenchman is now making a speech, so that instead of listening to him.

I am afraid that we have no chance for Kingston. We will however make a fight for it.

The French will I think be too strong for us & we must submit to going to Lower Canada. I regret this, but it can't be helped. Give my sincere love to Margaret & Louisa as also to the Doctor & believe me as ever my dear Mother,

your affectionate son

J. A. M^{c}D.

---

[54]This episode was a particularly nasty public outbreak of the long Brown-Macdonald feud. Macdonald had just reopened the old controversy by accusing Brown of falsifying evidence while secretary of a commission investigating the affairs of Kingston Penitentiary in 1849. The commission's report had been highly critical of Macdonald's friend, the then warden, Henry Smith, Senior. Macdonald never succeeded in proving his charges against Brown.

[55]Sir William Logan was the first director of the Geological Survey of Canada, 1843-75.

43 To Mrs. Hugh Macdonald

My dear Mother—   Toronto April 21, 1856.
    We are all doing pretty well. Isabella is as usual & Hugh growing very rapidly. He is quite tall now & is putting on almost a manly appearance. He has discontinued his fuss altogether.
    We hope the steamers will soon begin to ply. The Parliament will probably sit for another month & then we will look in upon you.
    Give my love to Marg' & Louisa & to the Parson. Always my dear Mother,   yours mo affectionately
                                                    John A. Macdonald

44 To Mrs. Hugh Macdonald

My dear Mother   Toronto Jan. 27, 1857
    Hughey is doing very well. There is every prospect of his soon being permanently relieved. The doctors say that he is in no danger & that all that is wanted is time.
    He is to be well fed & to take but little exercise until he is quite well.[56] Love to all.

                                                    Yours affectionately
                                                    John A. Macdonald

45 To Mrs. Hugh Macdonald

My dear Mother—   Toronto Feb. 4, 1857
    I write hurriedly to say that Hughey is getting on very well. He has daily attacks of pain but they are diminishing in amount of suffering, & his strength is on the whole increasing. D' Telfer hopes that ere long he will be finally relieved.
    Hughey has now got a schoolmaster, who gives him an hour every day. He likes it much. In the spring he will get an hour more. Isabella & I are as usual. Love to all the household. Always my dear Mother,
                                                    yours affectionately
                                                    John A. Macdonald

---

[56]Hugh's illness (rheumatic fever?) lasted for some months.

My dear James,   *Toronto Feb. 13, 1857*
    I had a note from Louisa yesterday, but not one line from Kingston today, if you knew how anxious I am you would spare five minutes to gratify me, however I do my best to keep up my spirits by calling to mind, that no news is good news.
    Hugh is sitting up today but is not dressed. Isabella is not worse than she was yesterday but John is almost entirely without the power of moving.[57] Dr. Telfer says that severe as the pain is it will be gone in a few days and he will then be able to move about. I see I have forgotten to tell you that the pain is in his back, brought on by severe coughing, it began yesterday morning and before night his shoulders and legs were affected, he is very nearly helpless, the palpitation has gone off but he takes no food, he drinks a little milk. Give my love to my Mother, if she could she would write to me. As for you and Louisa I dont care a button about you. If I do not get a letter from home tomorrow I shall not speak to either of you when I return, but I cannot bring myself to think so badly of you. In good hope of getting a letter tomorrow I think I can with truth, even yet, subscribe myself,

                                                affectionately yours
                                                M.W.
I am writing on my lap.

My dear Louisa   *Toronto March 17, 1857*
    We are now busily engaged in the House of Assembly discussing the question of the Seat of Government, on which we expect a very close vote.
    While Mr Papin is making a French speech, I snatch a moment to write you. My arm had a very severe sprain & I have it yet wrapped in flannel but it is nearly well.

[57]Macdonald, Isabella, Hugh, and their two servants had all had a severe bout of 'flu. Macdonald wrote to a friend on February 18, "had my sister not come up express from Kingston I really do not know what we would have done".

My health is very good & my strength fast returning.

Hugh is quite well, & now that the weather is getting warmer, we can allow him to play in the open air. Poor little fellow he was confined to the house all winter as the Doctor thought it would not do for him to go out, when he was obliged to take a hot bath daily. He takes a two hour's lesson every day and is a wonderful arithmetician. Isabella is, I think in very unusual health and strength. I think of going off early for a trip some where as soon as the House rises, & will leave Isa & Hugh at the seaside. Give my love to Mamma & Moll not forgetting the Parson.

Yours always
John A. Macdonald

48 TO LOUISA MACDONALD

My dear Louisa   *Toronto April 27, 1857*

I have got your note of Saturday— I have not been well this summer,[58] but am now much better, and my health is tolerably good. On the rising of Parliament, I intend to go to the seashore and not to England. I hope to have 6 weeks of seabathing, which will put me all right again.

Isa & Hugh are as usual. Love to Mamma, Moll & the Parson.

Yours always
J. A. M^cD.

49 TO MRS. HUGH MACDONALD

On board the *Anglo Saxon*[59]
My dearest Mother   *July 28, 1857*

I have just written Isabella & now merely send you a line or two to keep my promise. We hope to see the Irish Coast this afternoon & to arrive at Liverpool tomorrow night about eight oclock. We will meet the Indian tomorrow at sea & hope to put our letters on board. We have had

[58]Winter?

[59]Macdonald was part of a government delegation to England which hoped to arrange financial backing for an Intercolonial railroad.

a pleasant but uneventful passage. A couple of icebergs & a few whales being all our wonders. I escaped sea sickness wonderfully, a little squeamish for three days and decidedly sick one morning, but I never lost my dinner. A great a wonderful change for me. There are a good many people on board whom I know so that I have had no want of conversation or society.

I write with great difficulty as I am sitting just over the screw which shakes the ship & my hand abominably.

I will write from London & give the news. With warmest love for the girls & the Parson, believe me my dearest Mother,

your affectionate son
John A. Macdonald

50 To Mrs. Hugh Macdonald

My dearest Mother   *London July 31, 1857*

We thought we could put letters on board the "Indian" on her way out & with that expectation I wrote you the enclosed, but we missed her.

We (Rose[60] & I) arrived at Liverpool on Wednesday night.

On Thursday we came up here. Last night we went to the opera, and this morning I am up to the eyes in business. I have already seen Chief Justice Draper & John Ross,[61] & go to hunt up Sir Edmund Head this afternoon. I wont be able to see John Clark or Evan till tomorrow. Love again to all yr household.

Yours affectionately
John A. Macdonald

[60]Sir John Rose (1820-88), successful Montreal lawyer, was an old friend whom Macdonald had persuaded to enter politics in the general election of that year. He was to be the first federal Minister of Finance, 1867-9, before leaving Canada to live in England.
[61]William Henry Draper was in England to uphold Canada's claim to the Hudson's Bay Company territories in the Northwest. Ross was at this time president of the Grand Trunk Railway.

My dearest Mother–   *London August 11, 1857*
    I am glad to learn from the letters I have received today, that you are all well in Canada. I am, thank God! in good health and spirits & enjoying myself amazingly.
    Rose is a pleasant companion and we get on very well together.
    I dined with Evan & his wife the other day. He is in wonderfully good preservation, but his wife appears to be delicate. John & William Clark are both in the country, but I hope to see them before I return. You will have been glad to learn that there is nothing serious the matter with Jimmy Macpherson according to the opinion of the medical men here, and that a few years attention to his health will completely restore him.[62] He has just gone north to Catharine. Tom Gardyne will be with you in a short time. I think he sails next Saturday for America. He seems to be a nice lively lad.[63] I must write to Isa and therefore can give you no long yarn about my doings. I think I must reserve that till my return. Give all sorts of love to Moll, Louisa & the Parson & believe me my dear Mother,

                                                    yours alwys
                                                    John A. Macdonald

My dearest Mother   *London Aug. 21, 1857*
    I wrote Isabella three days ago, but must keep my promise of writing yourself.
    I am well thank God, & in good spirits. Rather tired of London & anxious to get back. I go to Paris tonight for three days. On my return I intend to visit John & William Clark who both live in the country, tho' far apart & hope to sail on the 9th September. I have seen a good deal of Evan & his wife. They also go to the country in a day or two.

---

[62]James Pennington Macpherson, Maria Macpherson's second son, regained his health, lived to be seventy-seven and to write a two-volume biography of Sir John A. Macdonald, which he published in 1893.
[63]Thomas M. Bruce Gardyne, son of Macdonald's cousin Catherine Macpherson, was emigrating to Canada.

I have ordered a Highland dress for Hugh, & have no doubt he will bare his bottom with due Celtic dignity. I must reserve all adventures until my return. Give all sorts of love to Moll, Loo & the Parson. Kiss Hugh for me,

alwys your affectionate son
J.A.MD.

53 To Mrs. Hugh Macdonald

My dearest Mother   *Toronto Nov. 30, 1857*
    We had a pleasant run up the railway yesterday and got comfortably to the Rossin House[64] last night about half past nine. Mr Rose of Montreal and other gentlemen of my acquaintance were in the cars, so I had lots of people to talk to on the way. By the way Tom Rae was on board looking very red and pursy. I have not yet received a telegraph telling me how you are, but expect one every moment. Love to yr household.

Alwys, Yours affectionately
John A. Macdonald

[64]The Rossin House, at the south-east corner of York and King streets, had only recently been opened. It was the largest and finest hotel in Toronto, until it burned in 1860. It was later rebuilt.

PART TWO ❧ 1858-1878

Before 1858, John A. Macdonald's life was a fairly steady progress to a
position of power; after 1878, it fell more and more into a regular pattern.
But the twenty years between were full of great achievement and of frus-
tration and despair. They were years of massive and rapid political change.
In the dying days of the old United Province of Canada, Macdonald, as
party leader, revealed all the skill in the management of men and affairs
for which he was to become so famous. He kept a loosely organized party
intact and usually in power through the disastrous election of 1857-8,
the successful election of 1861, and the doubtful election of 1863. He was
a reluctant and late convert to the idea of Confederation in 1864 (though
he had paid lip service to the principle since 1858) and his entry into the
Great Coalition, formed in that year to seek a union of British North
America, was also reluctant and in the end entirely practical. He did
not wish to relinquish power. "I had the option," he wrote in 1866, "of
forming a coalition government or of handing over the administration of
affairs to the Grit Party for the next ten years."

Once he was committed to confederation, his contribution to its
cause was of a very high order. It is arguable that he, more than any other
individual, made Confederation happen. He drafted almost all of what
was to be Canada's constitution. "I have no help," he told James Gowan
after the Quebec Conference, "not one man of the Conference (except
Galt on finance) had the slightest idea of constitution making. Whatever
is good or ill in the Constitution is mine." He took the leading part in
having his creation ratified by four provinces at Quebec, he chaired the
meetings in London that determined its final form. He was chosen, among
all other British North American politicians, to lead the new nation as

its first prime minister, to choose the paths that Canada would follow.

He had expected to be prime minister for some time, at least since 1865,[1] and he knew the direction in which he wished his infant government to go. He had never liked the idea of a federal union; he wanted a strong unitary system that would avoid the errors of the Americans with their tendency towards "states rights". He would see to it that the Canadian union did not suffer from the same weakness. "You if spared the ordinary age of man, will see both local parliaments and governments absorbed by the general power," Macdonald wrote to M. C. Cameron in 1864. "This is as plain to me as if I saw it accomplished."[2] He was wrong. He was to spend the rest of his life finding out how deeply, fundamentally wrong he was about the nature of the Canadian union. "Local parliaments" would not wither but would grow, at a surprising speed. Even before the railway scandal that precipitated him out of office in 1873 it was clear that many Canadians, including a majority from his own province of Ontario, believed in "provincial" rights.

If Canada was never to be the near-monolithic state that Macdonald envisaged, it was through no fault of his. He laboured mightily to bring into being a strong, united country, a rival to the United States. And while at first he succeeded only in creating a country that was large and a little truculent, still he literally built the nation, by cajoling and bribing new provinces into union, and old ones into acquiescence. When he left office in 1873 Canada had already achieved "Dominion from sea to sea", among other reasons simply because John A. Macdonald wanted it to and that he optimistically assumed (as he so often assumed about his private affairs) that everything would work out all right in the end.

By 1873 it was all too clear that Macdonald's own interests were not going to turn out for the best. They had turned out, in fact, very badly indeed. A hustling, ambitious, young lawyer named A. J. Macdonnell had become his law partner in 1855 and had quickly become an energetic professional and political lieutenant who had a helpfully wide circle of acquaintances. The firm seemed in capable, hard-working hands; the busy politician could pursue his public career undisturbed. But Macdonnell, even more than his partner, was given to optimistic, even grandiose speculations. When he died suddenly in 1864, the roof rapidly fell in on John A. Macdonald.

[1]Macdonald Papers, Vol. 293, p. 133955. Macdonald to Philip M. M. S. Vankoughnet, October 15, 1865.
[2]Macdonald Papers, Letterbook 7, p. 77. Macdonald to Cameron, December 19, 1864.

The firm's affairs were in chaos. Both partners, especially Macdonnell, had been deeply in debt. Responsibility for this debt, including the
cost of a number of railway locomotives which Macdonnell had bought
without his partner's knowledge and which no one wanted to buy, was
suddenly Macdonald's. He was broke. He could not even pay his insur-
ance premiums, let alone large debts. It would be years before the tangled
state of the partnership was even roughly sorted out. As late as 1881
Macdonnell's estate still owed Macdonald over $41,000.[3]

He tried sporadically and half-heartedly to do something about his
situation but he never had enough time. In the end, the burden of debt
came unmistakably home to roost. The Commercial Bank, to which he
owed most (though by no means all) of his debt, failed in 1867. He
reached a settlement with the bank's creditors which left him a poor man.

Power and affluence were gone; but by 1873 he had touched bottom
and his luck began to change. In the previous year a group of sympathetic
friends had set up a trust fund to provide him and his family with a
measure of security. He moved his law practice to Toronto in 1875 and,
though the firm did not at once prosper as he had hoped, at least it was
not a liability. He began to spend long summer holidays on the St. Lawrence at Rivière du Loup, resting, "recruiting" as he put it, for the come-
back which he was carefully planning. His old buoyancy returned.
"When fortune empties her chamberpot on your head," he advised his
friend, T. C. Patteson, "smile – and say 'we are going to have a Summer
shower'." The Conservative Party had been badly demoralized by the
circumstances of Macdonald's fall from power. It had been all too clear
that the prime minister and his close associates had gladly accepted large
campaign donations from a man who badly wanted things the government had to give – a charter for a Pacific railway and the presidency of
the railway company. Macdonald had to make the party and the people
forget those circumstances, forget that he had ever asked for "another
ten thousand". The times were favourable. The Liberals had taken office
on the heels of a serious depression which they had notably failed to
cure. But Macdonald left nothing to chance. The party was thoroughly
reorganized, mainly under the direction, ironically enough, of John A.
Macdonnell, the son of Macdonald's late partner, whose energy matched
and whose efficiency exceeded his father's. In dark economic days the
party and its leader took on an optimistic image. Massive conventions in

[3]Ibid., Vol. 542, p. 256565.

Toronto and endless political meetings and picnics across the nation carried a message of hope to the people. Macdonald had divined a wave of economic nationalism sweeping central Canada. Canada's industries had to be strengthened, protected against the powerful competition of the United States, if good times were to return. For twenty years Macdonald had been calling himself, off and on, a protectionist. Now he became one in earnest. "The welfare of Canada," he told his countrymen in March 1878, "requires the adoption of a National Policy". The "National Policy", the policy of high tariffs, carried him, in a landslide victory, back into the office he was to occupy for the rest of his life.

My dear Margaret   *Toronto March 20, 1858*
    I was very unwell last week so as to be confined to bed for three days and was hardly able to crawl to the House, when it opened, but I am fast rallying and hope in a few days to be all right again. I went out on Saturday night to John Ross. He lives five miles from town & I had two good nights rest & lounged on the sofa all Sunday so that I came to town yesterday (Monday) morning much refreshed.
    We are having a hard fight in the House & will beat them in the votes, but it will, I think end in my retiring as soon as I can with honour. I find the work & annoyance too much for me. This is a secret however. I can have no objection to Hughs becoming a dancer. Give Louisa the money for household expenses.
    Give my love to Mamma Louisa & Hughy. Kiss him for me & tell him to send me a drawing or rather painting.
                              Affectionately yours
                              John A. Macdonald
Love to the Parson.

55 To James Williamson

My dear Sir,   *Toronto Mar. 22, 1858*
Private
    I will try what I can do for the Observatory, but the Provincial Chest is so low that I am afraid Cayley[1] will shake his head at a new Grant. If I did not send you Logan's maps, I will do so.
    My speech told well in the House. It was difficult to strike out a new line after a three weeks debate. Love to all.
                              Faithfully yours
                              John A. Macdonald
P.S. Tell Margt I will go down on Saturday next.

[1]William Cayley, Inspector General of Canada, 1845-8 and 1854-8.

My dearest Mother   Toronto April 4, 1858
    I hope that this letter will find you as usual.
    I had hoped to get down for a day, but have hitherto been prevented.
I trust that ere long I may be able to gratify my cherished desire to pay
you a visit. To show you that the whole world is not ungrateful, I send
you two notes, one from the Hon Mr Chauveau Chief Superintendent of
Education in Lower Canada, the other from an old soldier for whom I got
a Company in the 100th. With all sorts of love to Hugh & the Household.
Believe me my dear Mother,

                                                    your affectionate son
                                                    John A. Macdonald

57 To Mrs. Hugh Macdonald

My dearest Mother   Toronto June 17, 1858
    You must give Louisa a good scolding for me, for not writing me how
you are and how you have been for the last week. Margaret used to correspond with me once a week. So tell Loo to be sure to send me a line. We
are getting on very slowly in the House and it is very tiresome.
    I hope we will get through the Session early in July & then I will be
able to go down to see you all. I long to hear of Margaret and her party.
Not one word have I had of any of you. Goodbye my dear Mother. I have
just made one speech & am about to make another. Love to Loo. Always
my dearest Mother,

                                                    yr affectionate son.
                                                    John

58 To Mrs. Hugh Macdonald

My dearest Mother   Toronto Oct. 20, 1858
    I was delighted to learn from Dr Dickson's telegraph that you have
got over your attack and are as usual. Now that the cool weather is
coming on I trust you wont be worried again with your foot.

You have heard me speak of poor George Hall who died last year. He was Judge at Peterboro and a warm personal friend of mine.[2]

He was reading this little book I send you just before he died, and he told his wife to send it me.

I thought perhaps you would like to see it. I send it to you by James.

I shall go right through Kingston to Montreal on Monday without stopping but shall pay you a visit on my way back. I only got a glimpse of Professor Williamson. I called on Dr Lawson[3] & left my card & went several times to the Rossin House to find them but without success.

Love to all. Believe me my dear Mother,

yrs mo affectionately,
John A. Macdonald

59 TO MARGARET WILLIAMSON

My dear Margaret   *Toronto July 7, 1859*

You will see by the papers what a narrow escape we had.[4] None of the party will again be nearer their graves until they are placed in them. The people behaved well, the women heroically.

[2]George B. Hall was a prominent Peterborough lawyer and lumberman. He represented Northumberland North in the Legislative Assembly, 1844-7, and was appointed (by Macdonald) Judge of Peterborough in 1856. Macdonald administered Hall's estate after his friend's death and arranged for the education of the Hall children. In 1860 there was a rumour, which may have originated with Mrs. Hall, that Macdonald and she were to be married.

[3]Professor Williamson and his colleague, Dr. George Lawson, Professor of Chemistry at Queen's, were in Toronto on university business.

[4]A week before, Macdonald had gone on an excursion on the steamer *Ploughboy* from Collingwood to Sault Ste. Marie. For some reason, the *Ploughboy's* cross-heads snapped in half, making it necessary to stop the engines, and the steamer, drifting helplessly in a heavy gale, was miraculously saved from breaking up on the rocks near Cabot Head on the northern tip of the Bruce Peninsula, when the anchor caught and held, forty-five yards from shore. A number of Macdonald's friends and political colleagues, including Philip Vankoughnet, John Ross, John Rose, John Hillyard Cameron, and Angus Morrison were also on board.

I am none the worse of the trip. The Governor General will be here tonight and I hope then free in a few days to get away to Kingston.

Love to Mamma, Hughy and Loo not forgetting the Parson.

Yours always
John A.

I send you specimens of the letters of congratulation[5] I got

60 To Louisa Macdonald

My dear Louisa   *Kingston August 10, 1859*

In case of your surviving me, I desire that you should dispose of the property held in Trust by C. S. Ross and A. J. Macdonell[6] [*sic*] as follows—

No decision to be made until after my mother's death, then you will keep £75 per annum for yourself and pay £75 to Margaret annually and to pay also to her annually what she may want for Hughey until he becomes 21 years of age.

In case you survive Magt you are to take for yourself £100 a year & the guardianship of Hugh until 21. When he becomes 21, the capital to be divided. You & Margt each to get what as capital will produce £75 a year at the then current rate of interest & the balance to go to Hugh, if when he becomes 21 only one of you girls survive, the capital to be given to the survivor to produce £100 per annum & he to get the balance. Should he die before 21, the whole trust money to be divided between you and Margaret or to go to the survivor.

No division of the capital to be made after my death till Hugh becomes 21 or dies.

Yours always
John A. Macdonald

[5]He sent three letters which expressed gratitude that he had been saved from drowning.

[6]Charles S. Ross was cashier of the Commercial Bank in Kingston. Archibald John Macdonnell was Macdonald's law partner. Macdonald's letters often refer to him as "A.J." or "Archy John".

61 To Louisa Macdonald

My dear Louisa   Toronto Sept. 1, 1859
    I have just got your and Hugh's letter of the 29th. By all means
return with the Macphersons, if you are ready and do not wait for me.
    I am kept here by the removal to Quebec[7] and my movements are
uncertain. So come home without me when you are ready. Love to
Hugh,

yours always
John A.

62 To Louisa Macdonald

My dear Louisa   Quebec Oct. 2, 1860
    I have yours and am truly sorry to hear of your continued dis-
comfort. If I understand the thing rightly the Lease of the House &
grounds from Mrs MacKenzie is to me.[8]
    If this is so the best way would be for the Professor to lease the
premises & you to pay him whatever expense he has been put to. If I am
wrong & he leases the grounds then you should make some arrange[t] by
which you leave & look out for a house. Do this at once & let me know
exactly the terms of your bargain.

Yours faithfully
John A. Macdonald

In great haste

Love to all

63 To Louisa Macdonald

My dear Louisa   Quebec Oct. 18, 1860
    If Hugh wants the Shetland pony let him have it. A. J. & I will settle
the price, but Hugh must ride every day. When it rains let him wear the

---

[7]The seat of government was moving again. It remained at Quebec until 1865 and
then moved again, for the last time, to Ottawa.
[8]In fact the lease of "Hazeldell", the house of Mrs. Sarah Mackenzie (widow of
George Mackenzie, in whose office Macdonald had studied law in 1830-2), was to
Professor Williamson. The house was on King (now Mowat) Street in Portsmouth,
west of Kingston.

waterproof I sent him, but he must ride daily. I suppose you got the increased allowance from Mr. McDonnell. I mean for the household.

I will send you a dft for $100 to be divided between you & Moll and on July 1861 I will give you the other $100.

Love to all,

yours ever
John A.

64 To James Williamson

My dear Professor   *Quebec Jan. 19, 1861*

Margaret wrote me some time ago that there was some difficulty about your allowing your man to harness Hughey's pony into his sleigh, look after the harness robes &c &c. Now I can quite understand that your servant has enough to do already, and I would not think of course of employing his services. When Mr. A. J. Macdonell was good enough to give Hugh the pony I thought it a pity that he should not use him till spring. He could not ride him in winter & therefore I equipped him with the driving equipage.

If not convenient to you I would ask you to be good enough to hire for me the services of some decent lad in the neighborhood who would look after the pony, and harness him for Hughey when he wants to drive. I should think there would be no difficulty in getting a lad for that purpose. If there is no lad to be got, I will, if you have no objection ask Mr. A. J. to take charge of the pony & sleigh. So that Hughey can go up there & get the turn out when he wants to show off his driving.

There are no news here. We have bright sunny weather. With love to all the household believe me,

yours faithfully
John A. Macdonald

65 To Margaret Williamson

My dear Margaret   [*Mar. 10, 1861*]

On getting your letter I telegraphed poor Louisa that it was all right to sign the papers. I shall however write Archy John not to ask her anymore, without first communicating with me.

Louisa might spend a week at Allan Mclean's[9] if she found herself comfortable after returning from Beamsville.

I have no doubt that Mrs McLean would allow her to be as quiet as she pleased.

The House opens on Saturday next, and we will have a stormy but I hope a short session. Until the result of the session is known – that is until it is over, all my plans for the future are suspended.

Entre nous, I think it not at all impossible that I will retire from the Govt this week. I will if I can, and be a free man again.[10]

Allan McLean is still with me. He is a very good fellow but rather ennuyant and I will be glad when he goes. I am now so much accustomed to live alone, that it frets me to have a person always in the same house with me. I hope Hugh's cold is allright and that he is back at school again. Love to all the household, believe me my dear Moll,

yours affectionately
John A. Macdonald

66 To Louisa Macdonald

My dear Louisa   *Quebec April 11, 1861*

I have your letter of the 3d April, and in the first place tell Hugh that I am extremely pleased at the report of Mr. May.[11] Tell him that I am quite proud of it and that I have shown it to all my friends. Let him go on & prosper and he will make his mark in the country yet. As to the proposed exchange from Portsmouth to Heath's farm all I can say is that which ever is agreeable to you all pleases me. You will have some difficulty

[9]Allan Neil Mclean of Toronto, an old Kingstonian, son of John Mclean, former Sheriff of Frontenac County. In directories of the day he is listed as "gentleman". In 1875 Macdonald's nephew, Henry Macpherson, married Mclean's daughter Eliza.
[10]Macdonald several times threatened to resign as leader of the western wing of the Liberal-Conservative coalition during the 1850s and 60s but always yielded, without very great protest, to the pleas of his followers that he stay on.
[11]John May had a varied career. After graduation from Queen's he became an Anglican minister, but spent much of his life as a schoolmaster. Some time in the 1870s he moved to Ottawa and was for ten years school inspector for Carleton County. For a short time he was principal of a commercial college in Ottawa. In the federal election of 1882 he ran against Sir John A. Macdonald in Carleton riding. He was badly defeated, but shortly after the election was given a job with the Department of the Interior at Winnipeg.

in moving Mamma, I should think.[12] I think the purchase is not a very profitable one, but I must get the calculations before I can advise. If it is intended to pay 8 percent interest — (which Romanes[13] charges) on the purchase money £1500, then the rent will be £120 a year, to large a rent I should think. Then will Mr Williamson be able to get rid of Mrs Mac-Kenzies house? Let me know all the particulars.

The House is still sitting but we hope to have a short session. Give my love to all the Household and believe me my dear Louisa,

yours very affectionately
John A. Macdonald

67 TO JAMES WILLIAMSON

My dear Professor   *Quebec March 13, 1862*
The Commissioner of Crown Lands is ready to report in favour of the College being allowed to purchase the land you write of, but the sale cannot be completed at present as the land may be wanted for purposes of fortification. A Commission is now sitting on the subject & they may report in favour of building a Martello Tower or some other work on the land in question. Love to all,

faithfully yours
John A. Macdonald

68 TO MARGARET WILLIAMSON

My dear Margaret   *Quebec May 23, 1862*
You complain of my not having written. It is true but I had the excuse of overwork. I have that no longer. You will have seen that I am

[12]The "proposed exchange" did not then take place. The move to Heath's farm or "Heathfield" was in 1864 or 1865, after the death of Mrs. Macdonald.
[13]The Reverend George Romanes taught Classical Literature and Moral Philosophy at Queen's, from 1848 to 1850, at which time he inherited a considerable fortune and moved to England. The Romaneses and the Macdonalds had been close friends in Kingston and remained in touch over many years. George John Romanes, son of George Romanes, became a well-known scientist who wrote on physiology and zoology, was a friend of Charles Darwin and founder of the Romanes Lectures at Oxford. John A. Macdonald frequently visited both father and son when in London.

out of office.[14] I am at last free thank God! and can now feel as a free man.

I have longed for this hour & only a sense of honour has kept me chained to my post.

If I had chosen this mode of falling; I would have selected the way in which we were defeated.

I have now fulfilled my duty to my party & can begin to think of myself.

I do not know when the House will adjourn but I hope to be able to run up shortly & see you all.

I have been very ill[15] but am crawling around. I intend to go down to Nahant[16] for a month to recruit.

You must have my room ready. I don't know when I may be up to take possession.

Give my love to the whole house hold & believe me my dear Magt,

yours affectionately

J.A.MD.

69 FROM MARGARET GREENE

My dear brother   [New York] *May 13, 1863*

Ann's address is as follows "Mrs. Capt Macpherson care of William K. Macdonald Esqr., Ovari, Lyttleton, Canterbury New Zealand".

She will be delighted to hear from you, you were & always a great favourite with herself and husband. I can hardly think of her as a grandmother, her oldest daughter has three children. I heard of them up to Jan. 8th, all well.

I was sorry to hear you were not well when last at home. I hope you will run across the Atlantic again early so as to be in England in the Summer and that you may be able to visit John & Wm. John leaves Brighton in July but when to he has not determined.

I hear so seldom of darling Hugh John since Maria went to Cobourg it is quite a blank in my life, my last letter from dear Margt he was well.

---

[14]The Cartier-Macdonald ministry was defeated on May 21, 1862, on Macdonald's own Militia Bill, which would have greatly expanded the Canadian active militia force.
[15]His illness was probably caused by a combination of prolonged overwork and prolonged heavy drinking.
[16]Nahant, Massachusetts.

God bless the boy & make him all you desire to see him, I can never be sufficiently thankful he is under such happy & salutory influence. Margt & her husband are kind & judicious in their treatment of him, & he is a darling, precious, promising boy.

In the last 10 days we have had very cold & 2 days of intense heat the trees are in full leaf, & Spring flowers & vegetables abundant.

May God bless & guide you my dear brother,

ever yr affte sister
M. Greene

70 To Louisa Macdonald

My dear Louisa   *Quebec Feb. 24, 1864*

On my way into town with the Professor, I spoke to him about Household matters, and we agreed that you should go on as you were doing and that things should remain as they are until my return at the end of the Session. So far so well, my present quarters here are comfortable enough. They are close to the House of Assembly, which is a great comfort on a bad day. My old house was nearly two miles away.

I was three nights on the road in coming to Quebec but I am pretty well just now, barring an occasional colic, which sticks to me with wonderful pertinacity.

We are now in the middle of the debate on the Address which will probably last all week. I have just got "What to do with the Cold Mutton" which I will mail to you.

Will you look for a little book, black with no letters on the back, Cavendish on Whist, and send it to me. Send to Mr A.J. McD., the big scrap book for 1863, and ask him to send it to me by Express.

Give my love to Margaret Hugh & the parson & believe me,

always yours
J.A.MacD.

71 To Louisa Macdonald

My dear Louisa   *London June 17, 1865*

Galt & Brown both sail for Canada today but I am detained for another week. I have a good deal of private business to finish and besides the University of Oxford is going to confer on me the degree of D.C L on Wednesday next.

This is the greatest honour they can confer, and is much sought after by the first men, so that I of course was only too happy to wait for it. We have finished all our work here in the most satisfactory manner, & in the way most advantageous to Canada.[17]

I have seen Dr & Mrs Romanes & go to see them today.

Tomorrow I spend at Strawberry Hill the house built by Horace Walpole & now occupied by the Countess of Waldegrave. I stay there until Monday morning.

I write in a great hurry & must bid good bye with my love. I sail in the *China* to Boston on 24th. With warmest love to Hugh, Moll & the Professor, believe me,

yours most affectionately
John A. Macdonald

72 To Louisa Macdonald

My dear Louisa   *Quebec, Aug. 23, 1865*

I have only time to say that I will gladly lend you thirty pounds.[18]

I have had Summer complaint, as it is called, which would not yield but to active treatment by the Doctor. I am now better. Atcheson[19] has been with me for a week. Love to all,

yours ever
John A. Macdonald

[17]Macdonald, Galt, Brown, and Cartier were in England to discuss confederation and the defence of Canada with the British government. Macdonald's account of the result of the negotiations seems curiously optimistic, since little was actually settled about either topic.

[18]He must have been hard pressed to find £30 at the time. In 1864 his law partner, A. J. Macdonnell, died suddenly and Macdonald gradually discovered that the firm was seriously in debt.

[19]Robert Shank Atcheson, a commissioner of the Trust and Loan Company of Upper Canada, of which Macdonald's firm was solicitor.

My dear Louisa   *Quebec Sept. 18, 1865*
    I will be up in Kingston within a fortnight and give you the money
you want. I would rather that there were no drafts between us. I was
very angry when I got Hughy's letter about the fire in my woods, but
Shannon writes me that no damage has been done. I must build my house
immediately, or I wont have a tree left.[20]

                                                    Yours always
                                                    J.A.MD.

                                        On board the Steamer *Victoria*
My dear Louisa–   *Sept. 28, 1865*
    I am on my way back from Ottawa to Montreal. I have taken a
House[21] there where Bernard[22] & I intend living. I want to know what
you have got in the way of furniture that you can spare me.
    There is some bed & table linen I suppose.
    Send me a list to Quebec on receipt of this. I attend the swearing in
of Sir John Michele[23] tomorrow. I then go to Quebec to pack up, bid good
bye to my friends &c & then on to Kingston about the middle of the week.
The Ottawa people gave me a great luncheon yesterday.
    I can scarcely write from the tremor of the table so you can scarcely
read this.

                                                    Yours alwys
                                                    John A. Macdonald

[20]Macdonald owned, or co-owned, a good deal of land at various points throughout
the province. These "woods" were most likely on the outskirts of Kingston, where
Hugh and James Shannon (who acted as Macdonald's Kingston business agent for
many years) would have known about them.
[21]Boarding-houses, such as Macdonald had lived in in Toronto and Quebec, were
scarce and expensive in Ottawa. The house he shared was on Daly Street, "the
West End or Fifth Avenue district of Ottawa" according to a contemporary hand-
book.
[22]Hewitt Bernard, Macdonald's chief clerk, future brother-in-law, former secretary,
and close friend. After Confederation he became the first federal Deputy Minister
of Justice.
[23]Sir John Michel, commander-in-chief of the British forces in North America,
1865-7, was administrator of the government in the absence of Lord Monck, from
September 30, 1865, to February 12, 1866, and again from December 10, 1866, to
June 25, 1867.

75 To Louisa Macdonald

My dear Louisa   *Ottawa May 28, 1866*
  Now that Hugh has turned Frenchman, I suppose that I shall be left in total ignorance as to how things are going on at Heathfield. You & Margaret must occasionally forget your farming & drop me a line so as to let me know how you all are. I send you part of a letter from the Hon Charles Alleyn[24] of Quebec, who was kind enough to look after Hugh for me there. McHugh[25] I learn from the enclosed telegram has gone down to see Hugh safely started from Riviere du Loup.
  He seems to have enjoyed himself at Montreal under the patronage of Joe Daly.[26]
  Poor Mr Atcheson has been at deaths door during the last week. He is I am glad to learn better.
  We had a great shock in our Household here from the awfully sudden death of John Galt.[27] He was our guest at the time, was in great spirits at breakfast and drove afterwards to inspect the Parliament House. An hour afterwards he was dead.
  With love to Margaret and the Parson, believe me,
                                      affectionately yours
                                      John A. Macdonald

76 To Louisa Macdonald

My dear Louisa   *Ottawa July 9, 1866*
  I am too busy to write you much. I did not go to the Pic Nic as I was kept in town by work. There are 4 McDonalds in Parliament and one of them doubtless was mistaken for me.

[24]Charles Alleyn (1817-90), a Quebec City lawyer and politician. He was Commissioner of Public Works in Macdonald's ministry, 1857-8, and Provincial Secretary, 1858-60.
[25]Hugh McHugh of Quebec City was Macdonald's former landlord.
[26]Joseph H. Daley was an old Kingston friend and supporter of Macdonald, who had helped get him a government job, as an emigrant agent, in Montreal.
[27]John Galt (1814-66), son of John Galt, author and first Commissioner of the Canada Company, and the brother of Alexander T. Galt, was, at the time of his death, Registrar of Huron County.

I suppose Hugh & John are having great fun just now.[28]

I shall enclose you Hugh's letters as I receive them. They will tell you I am well, if I do not write myself.

Yours faithfully
John A. Macdonald

PS.

I got the magnificent chimney or mantle piece cover & am greatly to blame not to have thanked Moll & yourself. I do not intend to *mount* it till I return from England, lest it should get spoiled.

J.A.MD.

77 To Louisa Macdonald

My dear Louisa   *London Dec. 27, 1866*

I sailed from New York on 14 Novr. There have been bi-weekly steamers ever since and yet I have not had a word from Heathfield, altho there have been 10 regular mails since I sailed. This is not right, had it not been for some business letters from Shannon, I would have been without any news from Kingston.

We have got on very satisfactorily with our work so far, & confidently expect a successful issue to our labours.[29] When I am to return however, it is as yet impossible to say.

For fear that an alarming story may reach you, I may as well tell it you as it occurred. Cartier, Galt & myself returned from Lord Carnarvon's place in the country late at night. I went to bed but commenced reading the newspapers of the day, after my usual fashion. I fell asleep & was awakened by intense heat. I found my bed, bed clothes & curtains all on fire.

I didn't lose my presence of mind, pulled down the curtains with my hands, extinguished them with the water in my room. The pillow was burnt under my head and bolster as well. All the bed clothes were blazing. I dragged them all off on the floor & knowing the action of feathers on flame, I ripped open bolster and pillows and poured an

---

[28]Hugh, now sixteen, was on duty with the Princess of Wales Own Rifles at Cornwall in anticipation of a possible Fenian raid. "John" was no doubt a schoolmate, possibly John Alexander Macdonnell, son of A. J. Macdonnell.
[29]The drafting of the British North America Act.

Helen Macdonald,
mother of Sir John A. Macdonald

Sir John A. Macdonald in 1868

A modern restoration of the study at Bellevue House, Kingston,
Macdonald's home from 1848 to 1849

Isabella Macdonald

Agnes Macdonald

Mary Macdonald,
from a picture taken in 1902

Hugh J. Macdonald

Stadacona Hall, Ottawa,
Macdonald's home from 1878 to 1883

Louisa Macdonald

Margaret Williamson

Professor James Williamson

Toronto June 17/58

My dearest Mother

You must give Louisa a good scolding for me, for not writing me how you are and how you have been for the last week – Margaret used to correspond with me once a week. So tell Loo to be sure to send me a line. – We are getting on very slowly in the House and it is very tiresome. I hope we will get through the Session early in July & then I will be able to go down to see you all. – I long to hear of Margaret's other party. Not one word have I had of any of you – Goodbye My dear Mother. They have just made me speak & I am about to make another. Love to doo. Always My dearest Mother Your affectionate son John

Facsimile of a letter from Macdonald to his mother

avalanche of feathers on the blazing mass, & then stamped out the fire with my hands & feet. Lest the hair mattress might be burning internally I then went to Cartier's bedroom, & with his assistance carried all the water in three adjoining rooms into mine, & finally extinguished all appearance of fire. We made no alarm & only Cartier, Galt & myself knew of the accident. After it was all over, it was then discovered that I had been on fire. My shirt was burnt on my back & my hair, forehead & hands scorched. Had I not worn a very thick flannel shirt under my nightshirt, I would have been burnt to death, as it was my escape was miraculous.

It was found that my right shoulder blade was much scorched, so I got it dressed and thought no more of it. In a day or two, however I found that it would not do and have been under the Doctor's hands for a week. The wound at one time took an ugly look. I was kept in bed for three days & have not left the House these eight days. I shall take a drive today, if the doctor allows it when he calls to look at my back. So much for that story. I had a merry Xmas alone in my own room and my dinner of tea & toast & drank all your healths in bohea though you didn't deserve it. I was to have gone to Evan Macpherson's to dinner, if I did not go down to William Clark, but I could do neither. The town is quite empty and I have no news to tell.

I shall know tomorrow whether I can have anything like a holiday, before the British Parliament meets.

Love to Hugh, Magt & the Parson & believe me,

affectionately yours
John A. Macdonald

I got all kinds of praises for the presence of mind and admonitions agt reading in bed. I still read however. Tell the Professor to write what he wants me to get for him. Prepay all letters

J.A.MD.

78 TO LOUISA MACDONALD

My dear Louisa   *London March 21, 1867*

Thanks for Margaret's & your kind letters. I have now been married some month & five days & feel quite as if it had been this day year. I have no photograph of Agnes taken here, but enclose you a very indifferent one taken at Toronto. It gives *but* an indication of her appearance. You will have seen by the papers that she and I were at Court and kissed hands.

Now you must understand that this was not a general levee or drawing Room where everyone goes, but a special court at which only those specially summoned appear. This took place at 3. In the morning at half past twelve, I and 4 others as a special honour had private audiences of Her Majesty. We went in separately. I went in first as head of the Conference. There were only in the Room the Queen, Princess Louise and Lord Carnarvon the Colonial Secretary. On entering the Queen put out her hand, on which I knelt and kissed it. On rising she said, "I am very glad to see you on this mission". I bowed "I hope all things are going well with you". I said I was happy to inform her Majesty that all things had been prosperous with us, and by the aid of Lord Carnarvon, our measure had made great progress and there had been no delays. H.M. said— "It is a very important measure and you have all exhibited so much loyalty". I replied "we have desired in this measure to declare in the most solemn & emphatic manner our resolve to be under the sovereignty of Your Majesty and your family forever" and so ended the audience.

She had kind words for all those who followed me. Cartier, Galt, Tupper & Tilley. Lord Monck is to return to Canada as Govr. General and has, but this is *entre nous*, charged me with the formation of the first government as Premier. We have been quite Lions here. My wife likes it from its novelty to her, but it rather bores me as I have seen it all before.

Tell the Professor that his seeds go out with Drinkwater[30] in the Great Eastern on the 23d next Saturday.

I saw poor Mrs Weir in London. She is in very low spirits at the opinion of Sir Roundell Palmer being adverse to her.[31] I am going to write

[30]Charles Drinkwater was Macdonald's secretary, 1864-73. He later became Secretary of the Canadian Pacific Railway.

[31]Mrs. Weir was probably the wife of the Reverend George Weir, Professor of Latin and Greek at Queen's, 1853-64. Weir was so quarrelsome while at Queen's that he was finally dismissed in 1864. He then sued the Board of Trustees for wrongful dismissal, but ultimately lost his case, in 1868. The Weirs were in straitened circumstances at this time, and later in the year George Weir asked Macdonald to get him a job. The nature of Mrs. Weir's case in England is not known. Sir Roundell Palmer (afterwards the Earl of Selborne) had presumably acted in his official capacity, as Attorney General, 1863-6.

to her to Scotland on the subject in a day or two. My wife & I dine with the Romanes's next week.

I am kept in England by some Canadian business and hope to be able to sail for Canada by the first week in April.

I shall go direct in the first place to Ottawa and afterwards to Kingston as soon as possible.

Give my warmest love to Hugh, Margaret & the Professor & accept the same from your affectionate brother

John A. Macdonald

79 FROM JAMES WILLIAMSON

My dear Sir John,   *Heathfield Jan.* 1, 1867[32]

Many thanks for your kind enquiries. I am happy to say, that I am now nearly quite able to go about freely without any trace of injury, and expect to be in town again at College on Monday. I owe my speedy recovery in a very great degree to Margaret's patient and unwearied care. I have been more under her kind control than under even the Doctor's orders, and I have just told her, that I am going to make a complaint to you, that she has been leading me a dog's life for the last six weeks.

It gave me great pleasure from day to day to mark the success of your conduct of public affairs in the first and critical parliament of the United Provinces. I am glad to think that you are now permitted to enjoy some degree of relaxation at least from your labour. I did intend to pay a visit to Ottawa during the Xmas holidays, but as it is I can only send to Lady Macdonald and yourself the best wishes & compliments of the season.

Private. I am anxious to know exactly, how it is to be with our College and Observatory grants for the last half year. Are they to be paid by the general or the local Government? And how are they to be received in future? I should suppose, with regard to the future, that it would be better for the different Colleges to have some plan for united action. It certainly would be of the utmost benefit to the country, when a high standard of education is so desirable for the more rapid growth of its prosperity, & the franchise is so low, to have the Universities liberally supported at different educational centres.

[32]Actually 1868.

One thing however, I want at present to write to you more particularly about. It is the Observatory. We have been doing a great deal of work in it during the last year and I wrote in the Fall to Sir G. Airy[33] under the instructions of the Senate with some of our papers for a set of the Greenwich Observations, a perfect Library in itself for our purposes which he has since in the kindest manner forwarded, along with a number of other valuable works, to Dr. Romanes for transmission to me on behalf of the Observatory. Now what I wish to say is this. I understand, that Mr Rose has included in the Dominion estimates[34] grants to the Quebec & Toronto Observatories. Why leave out, that of Kingston, a connecting link of great importance between them, the grant to which has hitherto been so small in amount, altho' absolutely necessary to the support of the Observer, the fulfilment of our obligations to the Corporation, & in short its very existence. The Observatories being a Dominion matter, and it is proper, that it should be so, that of Kingston ought to be included. The oversight can yet be easily remedied, and I earnestly trust it may yet be so. I am always, my dear Sir John,

yours faithfully
Jas. Williamson

80 TO JAMES WILLIAMSON

My dear Professor   Ottawa Jan. 13, 1868
   I have yours about the College grants. I am very sorry to see the course that events are taking on that subject at Toronto.[35] The General Government is, as you know, quite powerless in the matter, and I can only advise that the Colleges, whose interests are affected, should make common cause and bring strong pressure to bear up on the local Government. I shall write – indeed I have written to Toronto to my friends on the subject, but the local Government is very jealous of anything like dictation on our part, so I must act cautiously.

Yours faithfully
John A. Macdonald

[33]George Biddel Airy, Astronomer Royal, at Greenwich Observatory.
[34]John Rose, now Minister of Finance.
[35]Provincial grants to denominational colleges were cut off by the Ontario provincial administration of John Sandfield Macdonald at the end of 1868.

My dear Louisa—   *Ottawa March 6, 1868*
    I have duly read your letter. I cannot tell you how sorry I am for poor Mrs Logie.[36]
    I had intended to go to Kingston before the session, but could not manage it. Agnes will write you that we can't make room for you just now.
    The fact is our drain is stopped up and my study, where I do all my work, had so offensive a smell that it began to affect my health. Dr Grant[37] ordered me to leave it, and so we have shut it up.
    Dear old Mrs Bernard insisted on giving up her bedroom for my use, & took possession of her son's, and he, Col. Bernard,[38] is now sleeping in the garret. I hope that in another month, the frost will leave the ground, so that the drain can be opened & cleaned out & my room restored to me. Then I need not tell you that we will be too glad to put you up. Love to all,

                                        affectionately yours
                                        John A. Macdonald

My dear Louisa   *Ottawa June 13, 1868*
    I suppose you have Hugh with you, after his long labours during his session.[39] I intended to have looked in upon you today, with Agnes on my way to Toronto but was obliged to return here from Montreal on business. I shall go up probably by the end of the week. I am now living in lodgings. We have opened the drain at our House and hope soon to make it habitable again. It had got to be unsufferable, and the lower part of the House was almost useless. We are promised to have it

---

[36]Anne Logie died on March 10, 1868. She was the widow of Major William Logie, a prominent member of the Kingston Presbyterian community and a long-time Macdonald supporter. The Logie and the Macdonald families were very old friends.
[37]James Alexander Grant, M.D. (1831-1920) sat in the House of Commons, for Russell, Ontario, 1867-74, and for Ottawa City, 1893-6. He was created K.C.M.G. in 1887.
[38]Macdonald had in-laws the way some people have mice.
[39]At the University of Toronto.

all right soon again. Poor Mrs. Bernard went to Toronto, but Bernard himself stands it heroically notwithstanding all the smells and watches the house. Moll must be glad to have Hugh to fuss about once more. Give her my best love, & believe me

yours most affectionately
John A. Macdonald

83 To Louisa Macdonald

My dear Louisa   *Ottawa Sept 15, 1868*

I have been so very busy that I had no time to answer your last letter. I am quite ready to lend the Professor four hundred dollars for the purpose of making the repairs & improvements we talked about at Heathfield.[40] Let me know when the money is wanted, and I will send it through Shannon.

I have been in hopes of getting away from here for sometime. I think I can manage it next week.

Whelan the murderer of poor McGee was found guilty on clear evidence and sentenced this morning to execution.[41]

Pray give my best love to Margaret & the Professor. Believe me alwys

affectionately yours
John A. Macdonald

P.S.   We expect Hugh today

84 To James Williamson

My dear Professor   *Dec. 14, 1868*

I received your note of the 5th about College matters. Will you be good enough to ask the Principal to show you my letter on the subject as it contains my views.

---

[40]Again his willingness to part with his money is a little surprising. The Commercial Bank (to whom he owed, as it turned out, almost $80,000) had just failed. The eventual settlement of his debts, in 1872, left him literally wiped out.
[41]Thomas D'Arcy McGee was assassinated in the early morning of April 7, 1868.

There is no use in taking any steps whatever, until the prorogation of the Assembly at Toronto; after that Sandfield can do no more mischief by legislation for another year.

When our House meets at Ottawa he and two of his Ministers, Wood[42] & Carling[43], will be here, and I shall endeavour to convert them from their present mode of thinking. Believe me,

yours always
John A. Macdonald

85 To Louisa Macdonald

My dear Louisa   *Ottawa Aug. 16, 1868*
I received your letter with the check for $50. I hope poor Moll is all right again.

I leave here for Portland on Wednesday to spend ten days or a fortnight at the seaside. All right with Agnes when I heard last. I really do not know anything about James Macpherson's transactions with his mother's property or Reiffenstein.[44] Love to all,

yours affectionately
John A. Macdonald

86 To James Williamson

My dear Parson   *Ottawa Dec. 13, 1869*
I fear that I have been guilty of great negligence in not sooner answering your letter, but I laid it aside when it came as I was then very busy and it was covered up with a heap of other papers, from which it has only now emerged.

I greatly regret that you were induced to take stock in the Gold

[42]Edmund Burke Wood (1820-82) was both Provincial Treasurer of Ontario and M.P. for West Brant, Ontario. In 1874 he was appointed Chief Justice of Manitoba.
[43]Sir John Carling (1818-1911) was at this time Commissioner of Agriculture and Public Works in Sandfield Macdonald's Ontario ministry.
[44]George C. Reiffenstein, of Quebec City, sometime chief clerk in the office of the Receiver General of Canada, was James P. Macpherson's father-in-law. Macpherson married his oldest daughter, Miriam Clara Dunn Reiffenstein.

mining company and do not see how you are to get out of it. I am precisely in the same fix, having been induced by similar representations to take stock. I shall go to Kingston after the New Year and see what can be done for both of us.

All are well here altho' baby[45] is a great source of anxiety. Love to all.

Yours sincerely
John A. Macdonald

87 MARGARET WILLIAMSON TO JAMES WILLIAMSON

My dear James   Ottawa May 13, [1870]
The Doctor thinks John is decidedly better this morning.[46]

Since these two lines were written in less than five minutes the pain has returned so violently that Dr Campbell[47] has gone off for the syringe to inject morphine. However he does not think it will be a relapse. I will not write more until he returns.

Dr Campbell is not alarmed he says while the inflammation continues he will be occasionally troubled with the spasms. The one he has just suffered from was caused by too large a drink of cold water, which he is constantly craving. The doctor has limited him and as he is a good patient he will obey him.

I have nothing more to tell you, he is still in his office. We occupy adjoining rooms. On Monday Dr. Campbell said he might be removed to his own house, the relapse of Wednesday has left him so much weaker that it is impossible to guess when he can be removed.

Louisa is wonderfully well. I did not expect to find her able to stand the journey so well.

I intended writing to Miss Bridger[48] this morning but now find I have not time. Will you send this to her? for I am sure she will be anxious about matters here.

Ever affectionately yours
Margaret Williamson

[45]Mary Macdonald, born February 8, 1869.
[46]Macdonald collapsed in his office in the East Block on May 6, 1870, and was in critical condition for nearly a month, after the passage of a gall stone.
[47]"Dr. Campbell" is something of a mystery. There was no doctor of that name practising in Ottawa at the time. Margaret may simply have got the name wrong. Dr. James A. Grant was Macdonald's doctor.
[48]Jane Bridger, an old friend, was a teacher of music in Kingston.

Louisa wishes [Raftis] and the Frenchman to make up the fences in the pasture field.

I hope to have a letter from you this morning.

88 To Margaret Williamson

My dear Moll   *Ottawa Sept. 23, 1870*

Agnes & I arrived here yesterday morning from Montreal. The people turned out to meet me in a very gratifying manner. However, you will see all that in the newspapers.

I am now in very good health, and *nearly* as strong as before my illness. I hope by care and regular exercise I shall soon regain all my strength. I shall not do much work for some months, but act in the Govt as Consulting Physician.

We found your basket of grapes and letter awaiting our arrival – both very acceptable.

Agnes has kept you and will keep you posted as to poor little Baby. Baby has had a hard time of it, but if we get her home here safely, I have more hopes of her than I ever have had. The Pall Mall Gazettes were sent to me to Prince Edward Island. I have kept them all however & will send them on, so that the Professor may read, if his tastes lie in that way, the leading articles on the war. They are wonderfully clear and instructive.

Give my best love to Louisa, & the Parson & believe me my dear Moll

most affectionately yours
John A. Macdonald

P.S.   I shall have Hugh summoned home at once— He has had his "Outing" & must now go to work.[49]

89 To Mary Macdonald

My dearest Mary   *Ottawa August 25, 1873*

You must know that your kind Mamma and I are very anxious to see you and Granny again. We have put a new carpet in your room and got everything ready for you.

[49]Hugh had been to Fort Garry with the Wolseley expedition. He went back to work as an articled clerk in an Ottawa law firm.

The garden looks lovely just now. It is full of beautiful flowers and I hope you will see them before they are withered.

There are some fine melons in the garden. You must pick them for dinner and feed the chickens with the rind. You remember that Mamma cut my hair and made me look like a cropped donkey. It has grown quite long again. When you come home, you must not pull it too hard.

I intend to have some new stories for you when you come in the morning into Papa's bed and cuddle him up.

Give my love to dear good Grand Mamma and give her a kiss for me.

Give my love to Sarah too, and so good bye my pet and come home soon to your loving papa

John A.

90 To Margaret Williamson

My dear Margaret   Ottawa Dec 6, 1873

We arrived here safely & found all well, Baby's cold not amounting to much. I am completely floored with my cold and obliged to remain in the house, which enables me to answer my letters. I must ask you to send me Lord Ripon's letter.[50] I find that I should send it to my successor.[51]

I have thought of a way to keep a servant, when you have one and the wages are settled say to the girl, "Now your wages are so & so, If we get on well together & I find you with me say on 1 June next I will make you a present of say $10 (or any other sum). Now this is not binding on me & if we part before that date you will get your wages as agreed on & no more.

If you remain, it is my intention to make you that present, but it is to be a present entirely optional & not wages" Now as every month passes, the inducement to stay & not to lose the present increases.

Try this plan. Love to all.

Believe me affectionately yours
John A. Macdonald

[50]The Marquess of Ripon had been the head of a British Commission to the Washington Conference of 1871, called to settle outstanding differences between the United States and Great Britain. Macdonald had been a member of the British Commission.
[51]Macdonald's Conservative government had been defeated, following the Pacific Scandal, on November 5, and replaced by the Liberal administration of Alexander Mackenzie.

My dear Professor   Ottawa Feb. 24, 1874
   I have your note. I don't think the Govt. will attempt to take away the small grant for the Observatory. However I will watch the thing. The course of the Govt in holding the elections in the Maritime Provinces after those in Ontario & Quebec belied all their previous professions but was not I think unconstitutional.
   They shall certainly hear enough of this subject when the House meets. This is by far a more effectual mode of attack than mere newspaper articles.
   I have been laid up for 10 days with a bad cold which has kept me in the house for that time. Dr. Grant says the disease has spent its force but I don't discover any change yet myself. He says I must not go out for some days yet. Give my love to the Household. Believe me,
                                   very sincerely yours
                                   John A. Macdonald
Little Mary who is sitting beside me sends her love to you all.

My dear Louisa   Kingston March 16, 1874
   As you have made your will bequeathing me your property, I wish to leave this letter with you as a memorandum.
   If I survive you, I shall dispose of your bequest, so as to benefit those we are both interested in. If you survive me, of course your will in my favour is of no value. You should in such case immediately after my decease, make another will, so as to see that our sister Margaret is provided for for life and Hugh should be made your residuary legatee.
   I think that you should at that time consult Hugh and get him to frame a new will.
                                   Yours always
                                   John A. Macdonald

93 FROM HUGH JOHN MACDONALD

My dear Father   *Toronto Mar. 25, 1874*

    I have just received a letter from Shannon in which he says that he has handed you a policy in the Colonial Ins^ce Coy which has been assigned to me and on which you wish me to pay the premium. With my present income it would be almost impossible to do this[52] but as it would be most unfair to ask you to pay the premium on a policy of which I am the owner, I think the best thing I can do will be to re-assign it to you, so that you can either realize on it now, if the rules of the Company allow of such a thing, or if you prefer it, can assign it to trustees for the benefit of my mother and sister. By the way this brings up a question on which I intended to have spoken to you when you were here but I forgot to do so. You may remember that when we were last at Heathfield together you spoke to me of the disposition you intended to make of your property in your will. I have been thinking that it would be better to make one or two alterations, if you do not object, and to have the bulk of your property to my mother and sister simply giving me a trifle to show that I have not been cut off for bad behaviour. For if I am ever to be worth my salt, I can make my own living, while they will be dependent on what you leave them.

    Hoping all are well in Ottawa, I remain,

affectionately yours
Hugh J. Macdonald

94 FROM JAMES WILLIAMSON

My Dear Sir John,   *Heathfield March 28, 1875*

    I need scarcely say, that I sincerely sympathize with Lady Macdonald and yourself, and Colonel Bernard, in your recent affliction.[53] I do so the more, having myself had some experience of how good and amiable she was.

    You will by this time have received an invitation to attend a Banquet given by the Authorities of Queen's on the 28th of next month. Answers

---

[52]Hugh was now a junior member of his father's firm, which had been transferred to Toronto.
[53]Theodora Foulkes Bernard, Agnes and Hewitt Bernard's mother, died at Ottawa, February 26, 1875.

have been returned by a great number of the invitees accepting the invitation, and there will be a gathering from all parts of the country. Mowat and McLennan[54] are to be present, and the meeting, as you may well conceive, will be wholly nonpolitical. Do send a favorable reply as soon as possible. We have stood staunchly by you.

You will remember Dr Snodgrass[55] spoke to you about the Governor General having given Gold Medals to various universities & colleges, among others even to Knox College, Toronto, and to Manitoba College, altho' the latter is only lately set in operation, while none has been given to our university. It is hard to say, how this invidious distinction has arisen. The Governor General, however, I should imagine would at once and willingly remove it. You requested Dr Snodgrass to write to you while you were in Ottawa, and you would endeavor to get the matter set right. He spoke to me about it the day before yesterday, and I suppose you will hear from him yourself ere long on the subject. The suggestion to the Governor General however, would be but a fair one, and I have every confidence from his whole conduct in such matters, that he would with his usual liberality accede to it.

While I am writing to you, and troubling you thus far, might I ask you to endeavour to get the Reports on Geology, Surveys & Public Works, and Marine & Fisheries for the present Session forwarded to me? Many thanks for the Canadian Hansard. I am carefully preserving it for binding.

I am with best regards to Lady Macdonald, & yourself not forgetting little Mary, and the Colonel.

Yours faithfully
Jas. Williamson

95 To James Williamson

My dear Professor   Ottawa Apr. 2, 1875
    Many thanks for your note of the 28th.
    I have written to Dr. Snodgrass saying that I would endeavour to be at the Banquet but could not yet say so positively.

---

[54]James Maclennan was Liberal member of the House of Commons for Victoria North, Ontario, 1874-5, and the law partner of the Honourable Oliver Mowat (Premier of Ontario, 1872-96). He became a Judge of the Ontario Court of Appeal in 1888.
[55]William Snodgrass, D.D. (1827-1905) was Principal of Queen's, 1864-77.

I have also said to him that I would see what could be done with the G.G. about a medal.

I shall look out for you the Reports you mention. With love to all. Believe me,

Yours faithfully
John A. Macdonald

96 TO LOUISA MACDONALD

My dear Louisa   *Riviere du Loup, July 14, 1875*

We arrived here in all safety on Saturday night last, little Mary being an excellent traveller. She has gained much already but till her teeth are through she will be restless & uneasy.

I need not say how sorry I am that Margaret did not gather up more strength during your trip. I fear that at her age the recovery of strength will be slow, and unless carefully husbanded may never return. Now it strikes me that it won't do for either Margaret or yourself to undergo another winter like the last at Heathfield. The cold & worry will be too much for you.

I am therefore strongly of opinion that the idea which was broached last spring by Agnes is a good one. If you three would take lodgings in town during the winter at a decent boarding house, you would be free from all trouble and enjoy a thorough rest. In the spring you could return to Heathfield and enjoy a change of air without the expense of travelling in search of it. If the Professor thinks well of this, the sooner you make your plans the better.[56]

You should have plenty of time to look out for comfortable quarters, to arrange for the caretaking of Heathfield & your household goods & etc. I see you have heard of our carriage.

It is a snug low little carriage with one horse which some of my friends gave to Agnes, as we live a good way up town.

You must come up to us in Septr when we return & see Dr Hall.[57]

With love to Moll & the Professor. Believe me,

affectionately yours
John A. Macdonald

[56]Louisa and the Professor took his advice, but not until more than a year later, after Margaret's death.
[57]The Macdonalds moved to Toronto in September 1875, to a house on Sherbourne Street. Dr. Hall was probably C. B. Hall, M.D., then practising at the corner of Sheppard and Adelaide streets.

My dear Father   *Toronto Nov. 30, 1875*

If you have not already mentioned to Mr Patton my intention to leave the firm of Macdonald & Patton, it might perhaps be as well to do so at once, for I think I had better go out at the end of this year and start on my own bottom in the beginning of 1876.

This would make a cleaner break than a separation at any other time and besides January and February are generally pretty slack months in the borrowing line and my successor would have plenty of time to get into harness, before the rush of business, which always comes on in Spring, begins.

I have not yet quite made up my mind where I will hang up my shingle, but I am making diligent enquiries in several quarters and expect to have information which will enable me to decide on my future home shortly. I have only to add that, although I am grieved that we should part from any disagreement, I dare say it will be all for the best, for I can quite understand that it will be much pleasanter for you not to have me in the office and as far as I myself am concerned I feel confident that by attending carefully to business and making the best use of such talent as I have I will manage to get on in the world and keep my head above water. I hope too that you know that wherever I may pitch my tent I will always be both ready and willing to do your bidding and will always hold myself in readiness to advance your interests in any way in my power, for although I think you are acting in an unnecessarily harsh manner towards me respecting my engagement I have no doubt that looking at this matter from your standpoint you are justified in the course you are taking, and I certainly can never forget the numbers of kindnesses done to and favours conferred upon me in times past. I remain,

your obstinate but affectionate son
Hugh J. Macdonald

98 TO HUGH JOHN MACDONALD

Dear Hugh   *Toronto Dec. 2, 1875*

I have your note of the 30 ult. I have today as you wish mentioned to Mr Patton your intention to leave the firm of Macdonald & Patton & strike out a house for yourself.

He agrees with you that the end of the year will be a convenient time for you to leave, so that you may consider that as settled.

Yours truly
John A. Macdonald

99 TO JAMES WILLIAMSON

My dear Professor   *Toronto Jan. 9, 1876*

I am truly distressed at your account of Margaret's state of health. I have no doubt that everything will be done for her that care and kindness can do and we must only hope for the best. I am busy this week with several things, but if there is any appearance of danger, I will on receiving a Telegram, set all business aside and go down.

Be sure and let me know frequently how she is getting on or let Louisa do so. Believe me,

yours sincerely
John A. Macdonald

100 TO JAMES WILLIAMSON

My dear Professor   *Ottawa Mar. 11, 1876*

I need not tell you of my sorrow in the sad state of my dearest Sister.

She is my oldest and sincerest friend and has been so through life. I feel deeply for you. If I could be of any use I would at once go up and be with her. Let me know if you think I can. Hugh keeps me regularly informed of the state of matters. His letters allow no ground for hope.

Yours always
John A. Macdonald

101 TO LOUISA MACDONALD

My dear Louisa   *Toronto April 25, 1876*

I arrived here all right on Saturday night at 12 oclock. Little Mary has a bad cold but otherwise well. Agnes as usual. She was very much touched at Margaret's remembrance of her[58] and will prize the bowl doubly. I send you eight dollars. I think you said Nickle's charge at the cemetery was $7½. If so give the balance of 50 cents to Jane. I forgot to *tip* her when I left. Don't I owe you for servants money which you from time to time have paid for me? Please to let me know when you next write.

I have a short note from the Professor saying he has had a talk with you about future arrangements and that you were to write me on the subject.

I don't think it can be good for you to be left alone from day to day in that big old house.

You will be continually reminded of the loss of our dearest Margaret.

I think you should look out for some nice companion to whom a home would be an object. See to this.

Agnes is up at our new house every day watching the progress of painters and carpenters.[59]

We hope to have the house ready by the 10th May.

Always yours
John A. Macdonald

102 TO JAMES WILLIAMSON

My dear Professor   Toronto Apr. 27, 1876

Many thanks for your thoughtfulness in sending me a copy of your answer to the undergraduates.[60] It is nicely expressed and must be gratifying to the undergraduates.

I am glad that you and Louisa have already begun to talk of future arrangements. I shall wait her promised letter. Meanwhile I advise you strongly not to exhaust your strength on the farm. We are all getting old and have earned rest. Your place is paid for and there is no necessity of overworking yourself.

---

[58]Margaret Williamson died April 18, 1876.
[59]The Macdonalds were moving to a new house on St. George Street in Toronto.
[60]The Queen's students had expressed their sympathy on the occasion of Margaret Williamson's death.

Louisa & I as your brother and sister must see to your health and you must be open to our advice sometimes.

Always yours affectionately
John A. Macdonald

103 FROM JAMES WILLIAMSON

My dear Sir John,   *Heathfield Aug. 6, 1876*
    I enclose design for the monument[61] which I have received from Welch & Son.[62] They propose to erect it on a rustic limestone base such as you saw at the cemetery. Be so good as to return it, and say whether or not you approve of it. We shall be guided by any suggestions you may make. I have again carefully examined the specimens of polished Gananoque granite and am not sure but I would prefer it to the Aberdeen. I believe it would look better and be more suitable for the purpose. I leave the choice of the material however entirely up to you. If you say the Gananoque, it will be proper to let Welch know soon, that he may get the stone and prepare it in time. The Gananoque monument of the same design will cost $450.
    We are all well here, and unite in love to you all.

Yours truly
Jas. Williamson

104 TO LOUISA MACDONALD

My dear Louisa   *Toronto Aug. 14, 1876*
    I don't know whether the Professor told you that John Creighton[63] has awarded you eleven hundred dollars for your four acres.[64]
    If he has not, do not allude to the subject with him. If he speaks to

[61]For the grave of Margaret Williamson at the family plot in Cataraqui Cemetery.
[62]Edwin R. Welch & Son, Marble Works, Princess Street, Kingston.
[63]John Creighton (1817-85), printer and bookseller, Mayor of Kingston, 1863-5, Warden of the Kingston Penitentiary, 1871-85.
[64]Louisa owned a part of Heathfield, which she had bought from the Professor, for use as a kitchen garden. The evaluation was preparatory to the possible sale of all of Heathfield.

you on the subject say that he can pay you at his own convenience. He has written me that he agrees to the award.

Will you send me the letter addressed by me to yourself, to be opened after my death. I think it requires some alteration.

Agnes & Baboo[65] are at Cobourg & are to remain there till the 24th. If it continues very hot here & there would it inconvenience you if Baboo and her maids should pay you a visit for a little while? Let me know candidly how that will be. Has Hugh closed his arrange't with Mrs Waddingham?[66] Love to Maria & Joanna,

yours alys
John A. Macdonald

105 TO JAMES WILLIAMSON

My dear Professor   *Toronto Aug. 14, 1876*

I am in receipt of yours of the 6th with the design for the Monument. Before finally settling on this, I should like to talk the matter over with Col. Bernard who has a good deal of taste in these matters and who will be up here shortly.

I have your note of the 10th enclosing Creighton's award. I suppose it is all right, and if so it is quite clear that your place as a whole must be worth much more than you gave for it. Prices must rise in Kingston & the vicinity and the thorough manner in which you have improved the place must make it command a good price, whenever you desire to sell.

My wife & Bairn are at Cobourg where it is many degrees cooler than here.

Yours always
John A. Macdonald

P.S. Of course you can suit your own convenience in purchasing Louisa's lot.

---

[65]Mary.
[66]Louisa and the Professor moved into a house owned by a Mrs. Waddingham on October 1, 1876.

My dear Sir John,   *Heathfield Aug. 18, 1876*
    I mentioned to Welch what you said in your note. He would like to know soon what you resolve on after talking over the design with Colonel Bernard, as it would be desirable to have the monument put up before the frost sets in, and if the Gananoque granite is to be the material, it will take some time to prepare. The more I see of it the better I like it, but I have no strong preference for it rather than the Aberdeen.
    Hugh is better this morning, but the pain though abated still continues.

                                                Yours faithfully,
                                                Jas. Williamson

My dear Sir John,   *Heathfield Sept. 21, 1876*
    Now that you have got over your fatigues and triumphs of your Summer campaign, I wish you would let me know, as soon as you conveniently can, what design & material you would prefer for the monument. The design you & Col. Bernard select I am sure will be a good one. The material however is also to be considered. I mentioned in my last, that I was disposed to think from what I had seen then from another visit to the Cemetery that the Gananoque granite was the best. I am now quite confirmed in this opinion from seeing a large monumental pedestal and column of this material finished and polished in Welch's. It looks much better than the Aberdeen granite and is in my opinion the very best stone for the purpose which can be procured for beauty and durability. The Gananoque stone is to form the material for the monument at Montreal to Sir Wm. Logan, a sufficient testimony to its excellence.
    We would have been up with a small party to see you at Belleville,[67] but Louisa was unwell the day before, and the excursion had to be postponed. She is now in her usual health, and wishes me to say, that they

---

[67]For one of a series of successful political picnics that Macdonald attended that summer.

are nearly finished with the house. With best regards to Lady Macdonald, Mary & yourself, I am,

Yours always
Jas. Williamson

108 FROM HUGH JOHN MACDONALD

My dear Father   *Kingston Sept. 22, 1876*
      Allow me to offer you my humble and hearty congratulations on the magnificent reception you received in Belleville last week. I had fully made up my mind to be present at the demonstration in your honour but just as I was on the point of leaving Toronto I received a letter from Tom McGuire[68] asking me to attend to some business for him there and as dollars are not yet as plentiful with me as they might be, my greed for filthy lucre overcame my love of party and I yielded myself prisoner to the Almighty Dollar and remained in Toronto until Wednesday the 13th Inst., but had I known that the Pic-nic was to be on such a large scale and your reception such a flattering one I would have let business go to the devil and made a point of being there. There can now be little doubt about the Bay of Quinte being loyal to the core, and I should not wonder if the County of Prince Edward gave a good account of itself next election. I had my first hard fought cases of the Division Court on Tuesday last before Jas. A. Henderson.[69] They were of course trifling as far as the amount at stake was concerned but McIntyre, who was on the other side in both cases,[70] differed from me as to what the law was and we fought them out to the bitter end, and in both I am happy to say I was successful. I am afraid I will never get over my nervousness in court, but fortunately for me I only feel it when I begin speaking and it passes off when I have been on my feet for a short time. There is really no news

[68]A young Kingston lawyer.
[69]Henderson, formerly a lawyer with the Kingston firm of Henderson and (Sir Henry) Smith, now a judge.
[70]John McIntyre was not always an opponent. He had studied law in Macdonald's office, and was a staunch Conservative. See below, p. 127. He was Mayor of Kingston, 1878-9.

here at present – Stewart's[71] case against Britton and Price drags slowly on and I doubt if it will be ready for the Fall Assizes. He says he is going to subpoena Moss Cartwright, Edgar and you and show on what a rotten foundation the politics of Canada are based.

With love to my mother and Mary, I remain,

your affectionate son
Hugh J. Macdonald

109 TO JAMES WILLIAMSON

My dear Professor   *Toronto Sept. 23, 1876*
Both Bernard and myself like the obelisk which I return very much. Choose the Gananoque granite. Welch's price is I think $450. He told me that I could have my own time to pay. So you must tell him that I will pay him by degrees. My last pic-nic for the season comes off at Norfolk on the 27th. After that I shall settle down quietly till the session.

Yours always
John A. Macdonald

110 TO JAMES WILLIAMSON

My dear Professor   *Ottawa Mar. 29, 1877*
The appts. on the Geological Survey as well as on the Pacific Railway are made on the recommendation of the Ministry of the day, with whom of course, I have no influence. If I see Selwyn[72] shall speak to him, but I dont like to write to him.

---

[71]Dr. John Stewart was notoriously combative and litigious. He had been Professor of Anatomy and Physiology and Secretary of the Faculty of Medicine at Queen's but quarrelled so bitterly with his colleagues that he was dismissed in 1862. He twice ran newspapers in Kingston in which to berate his personal and political enemies. He ran in the first federal election against Sir John A. Macdonald and lost. His lawsuit against the Kingston legal firm of (Byron M.) Britton and (C.V.) Price shows him at his most pugnacious, ready to take on Macdonald and three other M.P.s, Thomas Moss and (Sir) James Edgar of Toronto, and Sir Richard Cartwright of Kingston.
[72]Alfred Richard Cecil Selwyn (1824-1902), second director of the Geological Survey of Canada.

We are bothering the Government a good deal just now. Parlt. will
sit until 20 April.

Yours always
John A. Macdonald

Love to Louisa

111 FROM MARY MACDONALD

My dear Father   *Toronto Oct. 12, 1877*
    I sit down to write to you in my Uncle's room. I hope you are quite
well. Your wife Agnes sends her love. She did not tell me to say so, but
I am sure she would if she knew it.
    I have a little dog that my Uncle gave me. Dear Father, when are
you coming back?[73] I hope you will be back soon for Agnes misses you
very much and says often to me "how I wish my husband was back".
    The house seems so dull and lonely without you and I miss my
evening stories very much.
    I have had a letter from Birdie May but I have not answered it yet.
I had a letter from my friend Miss Pitceathly. I hope you are having a
fine time down there. Agnes will be down to you on Monday. She is
going somewhere on Monday, but I dont know where to. Perhaps it is to
you, dear Father. I hope you are very well. Gally came back Wednesday
night, and I saw her Thursday morning. Believe me,

Your affectionate Baboo & daughter

(verbatim dictation)   Mary Macdonald
Oh! what a scrimmage I've made. I forgot to say anything about my old
hen. Sarah is very well and as chirpy as ever. That's all.

112 TO LOUISA MACDONALD

My dear Louisa   *Toronto Oct. 22, 1877*
    I was "starring" it in the west when your letter of the 12th arrived.
I have written Hugh to get you to sign a transfer of your 4 acres to the

[73]Macdonald was away on another series of picnics.

Professor. He will also show you how to endorse the cheque for $500. which he or you can send to me. Get from the Professor the date when he paid the first $500 and let me have it.[74]

I send you down the lease of the house which you can give Hugh to keep for you. I am afraid that as your second year began on the 1st October & you have entered on your second year, you must keep the house till 30 Sept 1878. Consult Hugh on this point.

I don't think the Professor should sacrifice Heathfield. Canada is entering I hope, on a new period of prosperity and property must advance in value. Meanwhile you can keep your present house which is quite large enough to suit you.

I am a good deal tired with my western progress, which has been a marvellous success. I go to Montreal on 30th for a day & then must abide at home till Christmas. After Xmas I think I shall spend a week with you, so as to be in Kingston on New Years day.

Agnes and Mary are well and both off in a cab this morning with Bernard to Leslies (the seedsman) to buy some young trees for our house and grounds.

The workmen at Hamilton gave Agnes a beautiful gold necklace the other day & she made quite a nice speech.

Yours alwys
John A. Macdonald

113 To Louisa Macdonald

My dear Louisa   *Toronto Nov. 17, 1877*

I have duly received the cheque for $500— I had intended to have applied your money on the additional water stock that I bought in your name, but instead of doing so I paid it up in another way. This will make you so much the richer when I kick the bucket. Now you see I have a thousand dollars of yours, which I will invest for you, as I find an opportunity of doing. Meanwhile I shall pay you seven per cent for the money as it is worth that to me. As the first payt. from Dr Williamson of $500 was paid on 11 Nov 1876 I owe you one years interest which amounts to $35— I send you a cheque for that amount which is your own money to be spent as you please.

---

[74]Professor Williamson was buying Louisa's land on the instalment plan and Louisa was turning the money over to Macdonald to be invested.

From the 11th Nov 1877 I shall pay you interest on the whole $1000 (one thousand dollars) which I have of yours. This will be an addition to your income of $70 a year.

Put this letter away among your papers as a statement of the transaction, in case of my death before you.

When I invest this money for you, of course you will receive the money from the investment & not from me.

I may run down before Christmas to give a help to John McIntyre[75] but dont say so to anyone. All are well here.

Yours alwys
John A. Macdonald

114 LOUISA MACDONALD TO JAMES WILLIAMSON

My dear James   Toronto [Jan.] 14, 1878
I received both of your letters this morning and I hasten to answer them.

From what both Annie and you say about the Shaw house there can be no doubt which would suit us best quite independent of the rent. I think I said what I thought of Fuller's house in my first letter to you. You will also have received my telegram by the time you get this. I do think it would be a pity to loose [sic] it as we would not get so large or comfortable a house for the rent they ask for it and the yard is a great comfort, and Annie says she does not think the sun ever gets into the yard at Shaw's house, so I suppose it will be all settled by the time I return home.

Will you be sure and speak of our going to Mrs Waddingham when you pay her on the 20th.

When I spoke to her in October I said it was from no fault we had with the house, only there was no room for your books. Altogether it was too small. I don't wish to have any words with her if possible and the lease will bear us out in what we are doing, but I would like to be friends.

I shall be obliged to you for paying the water account as it had not come in I forgot it.

Mary sends her love to you and Hugh. Do tell him to write to her, if only half a dozen lines. She is a very sweet child. I find her much im-

[75]McIntyre was running for mayor of Kingston.

proved, she uses her limbs a good deal more. The town is in a great com-
motion today with the meeting of the delegates of the L.C. they are going
to have there. Committees are formed in every part of Ontario so that
all will be ready when the house is disolved [sic].[76]

I am glad to hear that all is going well at home. John and I went to
St Andrews yesterday morning, and heard Mr Macdonnel[77] give his
people a fine doing up. Tell Mr. Smith if he wants a good ——[78] I will
back the Rev. James against anyone else he can come across.

Good bye my dear James and believe me your affectionate sister,

Louisa J. Macdonald

115 FROM HUGH JOHN MACDONALD

My dear Father   Kingston Jan. 22, 1878
Yours of the 19th Inst. reached me yesterday afternoon. I am very
glad that you and Patton have agreed to part amicably, as it will be much
pleasanter for all parties to have everything on a friendly footing. If you
particularly want me to come up to Toronto this week write or telegraph
and I will come, but unless you have some good reason for fixing upon
this week I would like to postpone the trip. Tom McGuire's mother died
last night, and he is so much cut up that he is good for nothing and has
asked me to look after his business for the rest of the week, consequently
I don't want to leave now, until he is able to attend to his own business
and to keep an eye on mine while I am away. If you consider it necessary
for me to go up to Toronto to settle our arrangements in a personal inter-
view, I will go up on Monday afternoon spend Tuesday with you and
return on either Tuesday evening or Wednesday morning, but if your
arrangements could be completed as well by letter I should prefer it, on
the grounds of economy. A trip to Toronto would cost me at least $15⁰⁰,
which I would rather save if possible, as at present ready cash is very
scarce and I have got to be careful. As I understand this offer made by

[76]The Liberal-Conservative Association of Ontario met in Toronto on January 15
and drafted a platform for the next general election.
[77]The Reverend Daniel James Macdonnell (1843-96) was minister of St. Andrew's
for twenty-six years. He had achieved considerable notoriety by being tried in a
church court for heresy, in 1876. He eventually won his case.
[78]Indecipherable.

128

you and accepted by me, it is to the following effect: I was to move to Toronto and take charge of the business, and in return for my services was to receive a fixed sum for the first year. At the end of the first year a statement was to be made out, and we were then to agree what interest I should have in the business or what amount I was to pay you annually for your name and influence. The time of our entering into partnership to be dependent on the General Election, unless you found it necessary to send for me before the election came on. Of course if you want me you have only got to write or telegraph and I shall go up on Monday next or sooner if necessary.[79]

I saw Henry Folger[80] this morning and spoke to him about your conversation with him. He told me to tell you that he had already taken steps in the matter and that he expected the money would be raised in a few days, so I expect this matter will soon be settled in a satisfactory manner.

What do you think of the victory in Digby? Will the Government meet the House or will they dissolve and appeal to the country at once? I should think that their followers will be able to read the signs of the times and that there will be no end of ratting next session. I hope Jones will be left at home also, as the effect of a double defeat in the same Province following so soon after Laurier's rejection by his old constituency, would have a wonderful effect.[81]

I hope my mother has recovered her health and that Aunt Louisa and Mary are well, and with love to all in which my wife joins me, I remain,

your affectionate son
Hugh J. Macdonald

[79]The firm of Macdonald and Patton was dissolved April 15, 1878, but continued under the name of Macdonald and Macdonald, with Hugh replacing James Patton.
[80]Of Folger Brothers, Kingston brokers.
[81]W. B. Vail, Minister of Militia and Defence, was defeated in a by-election, in Digby, Nova Scotia, January 19, 1878. A. G. Jones, who succeeded Vail as minister, was elected in a by-election in his riding of Halifax, January 29, 1878. Laurier had been defeated in a by-election in his former constituency, Drummond and Arthabaska, on October 27, 1877, but elected for Quebec East, November 28.

My dear Louisa   *Toronto Oct. 2, 1878*

Hugh reminds me that you have some money of mine on hand. I had forgotten all about it. Will you pay yourself $51.60 for the wine and ale & give the balance to Mr Shannon. Ask him to send it home by Montreal bank draft.

I am in good health but have not yet quite regained my strength.[82]

I have not got the Professor's letter yet. I shall reply to it at[83]

. . . .

117 To James Williamson

My dear Professor   *Ottawa Nov. 18, 1878*

I wish you would do what you can for Power & Sons Architects,[84] who tender for the new College Buildings. They are good architects & good Conservatives.

Yours always
John A. Macdonald

118 To James Williamson

My dear Professor   *Ottawa Nov. 20, 1878*

I saw in the number of Scientific American that arrived when I was at Kingston a cure for corns. As I am troubled with these things I shall be obliged by your copying it out for me.

We are all well here and enjoying clear winter weather. We hope to get into Stadacona[85] next week.

Yours always
John A. Macdonald

Love to Louisa

[82]The general election, which took place on September 17, had proved an exhausting experience. Though his party won easily, Macdonald himself was defeated in Kingston. The wine and ale bill was no doubt an election expense.
[83]Part of this letter is missing.
[84]Power and Son, a Kingston firm, got the contract to build the new (now the old) Arts building.
[85]Macdonald, once again prime minister, had moved back to Ottawa from Toronto. Stadacona Hall, in the Sandy Hill district of Ottawa, was to be his home until 1883.

PART THREE 1879-1885

"We have overthrown the Brown dynasty and the country seems to breathe more freely already," Macdonald told Goldwin Smith two weeks after the election of 1878. He was back, and he intended to stay for at least ten years to finish his chosen work of nation-building. There were things he wanted to do before leaving public life, and for the first time he began to feel a certain urgency. Suddenly – it seemed to happen in 1880 or 1881 – he was an old man. "I never saw John looking what I would call old until this time," Louisa said of her brother in May 1881. "His hair is getting quite grey." Beginning in 1879 he suffered from re-curring bouts of sickness, usually following the strain of the parliamen-tary session or (as in 1882) the general election. He had sudden, alarming collapses, one of them in March 1880, to the dismay of his fellow wor-shippers in St. Alban's Church. He took long summer holidays at Rivière du Loup to regain his strength and he slipped away "home" to England whenever he could, often of course on business, but also in the hope of "improving" from the change or the sea voyage, and to consult a London specialist, for it was only, as Louisa put it, "on the other side of the Atlantic where John could get the best advice".

In fact even his English doctor could find no serious organic disorder. He was simply wearing out. "What a nuisance it is to get old and infirm," he complained to Sir Alexander Galt, but with his habitual capacity for readjustment he came to accept the fact that he could no longer do as much as he had once done. The days of his impulsive speculations in land and his sporadic attempts to make his law practice pay were gone. Even during his period in opposition when he lived in Toronto he had neglected his practice there, and after his return to Ottawa he gave up all pretence

131

of active participation in the firm's affairs, beyond attempting to use his influence to procure lucrative accounts.[1] A series of partners were left to manage a practice that had finally grown moderately successful. It now provided its senior partner with a welcome supplement to his income, as always badly needed, for he had gone into debt again during his campaign to win back the prime ministership. His financial troubles were no longer acute, however. The trust fund, the law practice, and his salary as prime minister were enough for most needs – enough to permit him, for the first time since his early days in Kingston – to buy a permanent home. In October 1883, the Macdonalds moved into "Earnscliffe", a handsome three-storey house of Ottawa Valley stone, set high above the river, with a magnificent view of the Gatineau Hills. "Earnscliffe", especially after $7,000 worth of renovations, was private, convenient, and spacious enough to hold the succession of friends and relatives who came and went.

In many ways the Earnscliffe days were the happiest the Macdonald family ever experienced. Louisa and the Professor were comfortably established at Kingston. Hugh, his new wife and son, and Daisy were far away in Winnipeg but were apparently prospering. Most important of all, little Mary's physical condition slowly but markedly improved, through being "rubbed and pounded along the chief lines of nerve" by a German woman who was trained in the "Swedish movement treatment" and who had been brought to Canada by Princess Louise. "She is beginning to stand," Macdonald reported in triumph on Dominion Day, 1884; "we hope to see her walk yet."

"Debts and troubles," John A. Macdonald once remarked, "disappear like summer flies and new ones come." Some of his personal debts and troubles had abated, if not exactly disappeared, but there were new and alarming political troubles at hand. The election of 1882 was the last real triumph at the polls, and even that victory was partly achieved by a deliberate "hiving of the Grits" through the judicious redistribution of ridings. Macdonald wanted to use the rest of his years in power for specific national purposes. "My remaining ambition," he told Sir Charles Tupper in 1881, "is to see that our policy is not reversed and that the N.P. and the C.P.R. are safe from 1883 to 1888." He encountered growing opposition. The depression, which had lifted briefly at the time he returned to

---

[1]He could sometimes be extremely blunt about this sort of thing. "Poor Crombie at Toronto has gone mad and may be obliged to retire from business. If so I want the solicitorship of the Bank of Montreal at Toronto for my firm." (Galt Papers, M.G. 27, I, D8, Vol. 45, p. 1479. Macdonald to Galt, January 7, 1880.)

power, soon returned. The National Policy was not making everyone prosperous and the C.P.R. was proving highly expensive to the public treasury. He was often discouraged and began to dread the approach of each parliamentary session. "You cannot fancy the loathing with which I return to work," he wrote to Sir James Gowan from Rivière du Loup. Yet there was nothing else that he really wanted to do. And there was still the C.P.R., and the nation, incomplete.

No one worked harder for the railway than Macdonald. When at last it was done, late in 1885, it had been brought to completion by the energy and skill of its builders, by massive doses of federal funds pushed through by Macdonald, and by a rebellion in the Northwest which Macdonald, as Prime Minister, Minister of the Interior (1878-83), and Superintendent General of Indian Affairs ought never have permitted to happen. But the C.P.R. at least was "safe". The nation was united in fact, if not entirely in spirit.

In 1885 Sir John A. Macdonald celebrated his seventieth birthday. A few weeks before, in November and December 1884, large and glittering demonstrations in London, England, and in Toronto marked the anniversary of his fortieth year in public life. Forty years. No other Canadian figure could equal, or even approach, the length and quality of his service to his countrymen. It was scarcely conceivable that there had ever been or ever would be a time when he was not an inseparable, inevitable part of Canadian life.

My dear John   *Kingston Jan. 26, 1879*

I would have written before, but from your saying there was a probability of your coming up this month, I thought I would wait till you did come, as Jane could speak to you herself. If you remember last autumn when you were staying with me, you asked Jane, if you could do anything for her.[1] She said she did not know that you could then. You then told her to let you know, if any time you could do anything for her. Now to make a long story short, her husband Robert Appleton fell ill with dumb ague last October, and had to give up his place. When he got better in the beginning of this month, the work was finished, and he can not get anything to do, even at half time.

It seems they are increasing the number of gards [sic] at the Penetentiary [sic], as there is such a large number of convicts coming in, and Robert would like to be one of them. He is 35 years old, sober (he sighned [sic] the Pledge years ago) and honest. Dr Williamson gave a letter to him for Mr. Crighton [sic], but as there is more than a hundred applications, he will find it hard to decide, but Jane (poor body) thinks if you would say a word for them to the Warden, he would be sure to get the place. He is well known in the Bay (Portsmouth). Mr Chaffey[2] gave him a strong letter of recomindation [sic], when he went West, and Robert had worked with him for years, but that letter has been mislaid, by the persons it was given to, and Mr Chaffey is in B.C., so they can't get another for sometime at least. Jane tries to be as merry as ever but I see she is getting anxious.[3]

I am so glad Annie is down with you for a while, I am sure it will do her good, though I miss her running in, just to see if I wanted anything down town.

There is nothing here in the shape of news, that I hear, but Johnie will be sure to get it for Annie if it is going.[4]

I have sent down in Johnie's box, a cosy I worked for Agnes. I

---

[1]Jane was probably a maid or housekeeper.
[2]George Chaffey, of George Chaffey and Brother, forwarders and commission merchants, Kingston.
[3]Robert Appleton was appointed a guard at the Penitentiary July 1, 1880.
[4]Anna and Johanna Macpherson, the unmarried daughters of Maria Macpherson, and, of course, the nieces of Macdonald and Louisa.

intended Annie to have taken it, but with one thing or other, I could not finish it. I hope she will like it.

Do you think we will see you this winter, the people are asking me when ever I go out.

Give my love to them *all* and believe me

affectionately yours
Louisa J. Macdonald

120 To Louisa Macdonald

My dear Louisa   *Ottawa March* 26, 1879
I am afraid I have greatly neglected you during the session but it cant be helped.

We are all well here except little Mary who has had a series of colds & is very weak in consequence. I send you a note from Hugh about the Shaws of Dalnavert. Please send me an answer to the enquiries & return me Hugh's letter – our grandmother was Margaret[5]

. . . .

Col. W. Shaw, & after his death married our grandfather John Shaw[6] who occupied Dalnavert – The question is – what relations were Wm. & John the first & 2d. husbands, & was the 1st or 2d Shaw of Dalnavert?

John Clark told me in 1850 that I was the last representative of the Shaws of Dalnavert.

I want to write the man who has written a book about the Shaws. In haste

121 From Louisa Macdonald

My dear John   *Kingston March* 28, [1879]
I can't tell you how glad I was to see your hand writing again, I did not expect to hear from you, as I know how much you are engaged, but when your note come it gave me great pleasure.

I went over to Maria, to see if she remembered anything about our friends in the Highlands, but I knew more myself.

[5]A small part of this letter is missing.
[6]His name was really James.

135

Our great grandmother was a Mary Ross, (an only child) she had some money. She maried [sic] John Grant, who was of the Rothiemurchus family, that I am positive of, from what my Mother told us, and from conversations I have heard her hold with W. Grant on the subject. My impression has always been, that he was nephew to Rothiemurchus[7] (Maria thinks so too). They had five children, one son, and four daughters, Our grandmother Margaret, maried [sic] William Shaw of Dalnavert, (he was not in the army.) They had two daughters. After his death, she maried [sic] James Shaw. He was not related to her first husband, she spoke of him as belonging to the Kinrara branch of the Shaws. Our grandfather was out in 45. He was afterwards in the British army. Lord Seaforth got him his commission. He and my grandmother lived many years in Dalnavert, but it was as tenant. He payed the rent to his stepdaughters as thier [sic] Father had left them the lease of it. You say John Clark told you that you were the last representitive [sic] of the Shaws of Dalnavert but I think he must have been mistaken, as I asked my Mother, if there was any relationship between her mother's husbands, and she said no, and I never heard her speak of any of her fathers relations, but one brother, who came to see him, and one sister, who was married, but not in that part of the country.

Our grand father was also married twice he had five son's and one daughter, his sons was at school in the town of Inverness, while he was with his regiment. 2 of his sons were drowned there, Cathcart and Farquhar.

George and one whos [sic] name I forget, got commissions, and died abroad. Charles went to the West India's. He was a merchant there. He was rich. He wanted our Mother to go to him, as he never married, but she could not make up her mind to leave her mother, so by the time there [sic] troubles came on, they heard of his death, and they never recovered any of his money. Our Aunt Christina I don't remember her name, married some one that displeased her father, and our mother did not see her often, as she seldom came to Badenoch. I tell you all these particulars, as it may be the means of finding out what you want to know. Maria has a book on the Shaws. She says she would lend it Hugh, for his friend to see, but she would not loose [sic] it on any account. You of, course remember what became of our mother's brothers. Alexander Shaw was killed in a duel, he left one daughter Susan Gordon Shaw, who

[7]That is, to the Laird of Rothiemurchus.

maried [sic] a Dr King. She died in Jamaca [sic]. William whose likeness you have, died abroad, James died in the States, William and the Miss Macpherson, that afterwards married Sir D. Brewester were attached to each other, but were to poor to marry.[8] I hope I won't tire you dear John, but as I am on the subject, I will tell you all I recollect of my mother's family. One of our grand mothers sisters married a Col. Mackintosh of Balnespec. I am sure you must remember Mama speaking of them, one died young, and Mary Grant married a man of the name of Smith, in the States, it is an ugley [sic] story but her brother John was more to blame then she was.[9] She returned to the Highlands, before my mother left it. Maria recollects her quite well, she had no living children. John Grant served in the American war, when he returned, he settled in England, and married (the second time) an English lady, who had money. They had one child Penelope, called after his first wife. I have often heard my Aunt Macpherson and my mother speak of her, as her Father always took her with him when he returned to Badenoch. She married one of the oldest Baronet, his name has escaped me. I would know it at once if I saw it, or heard it. In the old Peerage that my Father had of 1818, his name is at the head of the list. Mrs Greene told me she had visited them, but they did not corespond [sic].

And now dear John I hope you will be able to make out what I intend to convey to you. The first time you come up, you can take a look at this book of Maria's it will amuse you.

I am sorry to hear Mary has been unwell. But it is the same everywhere, colds seem to take such a hold on one, that you can't get rid of it. Give her my love give it also to Agnes I hope she is better. Annie said she suffered a good deal from headach [sic] while she was down. Maria is a little better for the last few days, so is Johnie what she wants is excitement. She found it rather dull while Annie was away. She is anxious that her mother would go and live in Ottawa. Annie can't bear the idea of it neither can Maria so we will see who will beat.

Love most affectionately yours
Louisa J. Macdonald

---

[8]Sir David Brewster's wife, Juliet Macpherson, was one of several illegitimate children of James Macpherson, the famous Scottish poet and the translator of the Ossianic poems, which Dr. Samuel Johnson claimed were fraudulent. James Macpherson was from Badenoch, Inverness-shire, as were the Kingston Macphersons.
[9]Louisa is frustratingly vague about this. We shall probably never know the "ugley story".

My dear Louisa   Ottawa June 26, 1879
    I duly rec'd your letter and the cheque all right.
    I have also got my clothes, for which thanks!
    Agnes & little Mary left me this morning, Agnes for England, Mary
and her two maids for Riviere du Loup. By the way if you would like some
salt water bathing, go down to R. Du Loup. Sarah is Boss & will give you
a room.
    I am obliged to remain for a week greatly to my disgust. I send you
a cheque for $35 being the interest due you on 1 July. Don't present it
before that date. Love to the Professor.
                                                    Yours alwys
                                                    John A. Macdonald
Send me by return of post – Wm. Clark's address & Ann Macpherson's
in N. Zealand. Hugh wrote Ann for me. In England I will write myself.
Love to Maria & the girls. James' salary is now $1200 a year a good rise
from $800.[10]

                                                    J.A.MD.

My dear Louisa   Ottawa July 6, 1879
    I was sure you would be frightened by the paragraphs in the papers.
Agnes left Thursday week for England and Mary with her two maids for
Riviere du Loup. I was to follow next week afterwards. The day that
Agnes left I was attacked with regular cholera and it was accompanied
by cramps or spasms similar in character to those of 1870.
    The doctor took vigorous steps and has pulled me through, though
very weak. The servants have been very kind and attentive & I wanted
nothing. I expect to sail for England next Saturday. The Doctors Grant
and Tupper[11] agreed it would not be safe for Mary to go to sea & I was
very glad of it. She is much better at R. du Loup where she has Sarah

[10]James Pennington Macpherson spent many years in the Canadian civil service,
from 1884 to 1895 as chief clerk of the Department of Public Works.
[11]Sir Charles Tupper.

and Oswald, two very good women with her and Miss Reynolds next door. Love to the Professor

yours affectionately
J.A.MD.

124 TO LOUISA MACDONALD

My dear Louisa   *London Aug. 20, 1879*

You will have seen that the Queen gave me an audience and swore me in as a Privy Councillor. The *Globe* to the contrary notwithstanding.

I had a pleasant voyage across the Atlantic[12] and have received no end of civilities since, but I shall reserve particulars till my return next month. I have not seen Wm. Clark yet as I was too busy to leave town, but I go down this week. I enclose you two notes to show Maria.

Agnes has been enjoying herself immensely. She has two charming cousins here, Lady Barker & Louisa Scott.[13]

The three are very like and standing together they make a very distingué group.

My old friends are very true to me. Agnes & I have been staying with the Earl of Carnarvon,[14] who likes me much from of old, at Highclere Castle one of the swellest places in England. We intend to go to Mr Bouveries, son of the Earl of Radnor and instead of sailing from Liverpool shall go to Ireland & sail from Londonderry. This will enable us to spend a few days between Lord Monck's & Lord Dufferin's.[15] We have of course seen the Roses at Losely Park, a fine old place, belonging to the family of which Sir Thomas More, Henry the 8th's chancellor, was one, and we intend to visit Lady Lisgar at Bosworth Park.[16] It would amuse you

[12]The purpose of the trip to England was to discuss the building of the C.P.R. and the creation of a Canadian High Commission in London.
[13]Lady Mary Ann Barker and Louisa Scott were sisters, whose maiden name was Stewart. They were Jamaica cousins, the daughters of Hon. Walter George Stewart, Secretary and Member of the Council of Jamaica. (One of Agnes's brothers was named Walter Stewart Bernard.) Lady Barker was the widow of a distinguished soldier, Colonel Sir George Robert Barker, K.C.B., but at this time was actually remarried to Frederick Napier Broome, of Canterbury, New Zealand.
[14]The Earl of Carnarvon had been Colonial Secretary during most of the Confederation negotiations.
[15]The first and third Governors General of Canada.
[16]Lady Lisgar, widow of the second Governor General. The correct name of the estate was Bosworth Hall.

to see how Agnes swells it, & I like to see it. I had a cable message yesterday from Riviere du Loup saying that little Mary was quite well.

Love to the Professor and to all at Clyde Terrace.

Yours faithfully & affectionately
John A. Macdonald

125 TO LOUISA MACDONALD

My dear Louisa   Ottawa Dec. 27, 1879

I send you a cheque for $35 being the half years' interest due on 1 Jany 1880 on your $1000 in my hands.

Don't present it at the bank till 1 January.

All well here. We dined on Christmas with our old friend Reynolds.[17] I fear he will never see another. Love to the Professor.

Yours alwys
John A. Macdonald

126 TO LOUISA MACDONALD

My dear Louisa   Ottawa Jan. 27, 1880

Agnes went westward to Toronto yesterday and will probably be there for a week. She talked about paying you a visit on her way back. She will however write you on the subject.

I am sorry to hear of the Professor's state of health. Dr Evans should watch him closely.

Put me down for $5 for poor McKerras's[18] portrait.

Yours affectionately
John A. Macdonald

I hope you are quite strong again

[17]Thomas Reynolds (1811-80) was a railway man who was at various times connected with the Great Western and the Ottawa and Prescott railways and the Ottawa Horsecar Company. He had a summer place at Rivière du Loup next to the Macdonalds where his sister often looked after Mary. Macdonald's nephew, Edmund Dalrymple Clark, son of Major-General John Clark, married Reynolds' daughter Clara in 1879. Reynolds died the following June in Europe. In 1882 Macdonald bought Reynolds' house "Earnscliffe" on Sussex Drive in Ottawa from Reynolds' son.
[18]The Reverend John Hugh McKerras (1832-80), Professor of Classical Literature at Queen's, 1864-80, died January 9, 1880.

127 TO JAMES WILLIAMSON

My dear Professor   *Ottawa June 24, 1880*
    I send you a Fortnightly of November last which by some accident was not sent you. The June numbers of Fortnightly and Contemporary just recd.
    I shall be in Kingston on my way to Bath next Tuesday but you & Louisa will probably be at Westport.
    Agnes & Mary go to R. du Loup today. I shall be here for a little while yet to wind up business.

Yours always
John A. Macdonald

128 TO LOUISA MACDONALD

My dear Louisa   *Ottawa June 25, 1880*
    Thinking you were still at Westport I wrote the Professor yesterday. Sir L. Tilley & I will go up on Monday night to Kingston, sleep at the B. American[19] & go out on Tuesday morning to Bath. We will return on Tuesday evening, in time I hope to take tea with you and come down in the middle of the night so as to be here on Wednesday morning, so I shall only get a peep at you. Agnes & Mary with two women & Oswald's little Fanny left here yesterday for Riviere du Loup.
    I shall go down in about a fortnight. I have received the Trust & Loan cheque all right. With respect to the waterstock, we must keep it all. I shall pay for the new stock. It will make you richer, if I should pop off before you. At any rate it will make Hugh so much the richer.
    On the first of July go to the waterworks office and subscribe for all the stock allotted to you and subscribe for Hugh as well. By the way you did not send me Hugh's power of Attorney to you but you should take it with you to the waterworks office.
    Make the Professor go with you. Mr Wilson will explain to you what is to be done.[20]

[19]The British American Hotel in Kingston.
[20]Wilson was manager of the Kingston Waterworks Company.

Tell Wilson you will pay in such sums as may be called up by the Board.

Return me the paper signed James Wilson that I now send you.

Yours faithfully
John A. Macdonald

P.S.   I send you a cheque for $35 being the interest due you on 1st July.

129 To Louisa Macdonald

My dear Louisa   *Ottawa July 6, 1880*

Thanks for your note. I will attend to the water stock. It is better for Hugh to return the water stock as he has left Kingston. I sail for England on next Saturday the 10th and will be absent for 6 weeks or 2 months at latest.[21]

Agnes is here. She is taking down to R. du Loup Miriam Macpherson[22] & a young sick girl Miss Bury who is ordered change of air & her mother can't afford it.[23] I shall write John Creighton about Jane's husband.

I shall tell Agnes to write you from time to time as to my doings in England.

You must have been sorry to hear of my poor friend Reynold's death in France last week.

Yours affectionately
John A. Macdonald

130 Hugh John Macdonald to James Williamson

My dear Mr. Williamson   *Toronto, Aug. 23, 1880*

I send you today by book post the Bystander for this month, containing a short but good article on "Protection or Free Trade", which

---

[21]To negotiate a C.P.R. contract.
[22]Daughter of James P. Macpherson.
[23]Ada Pierce Tighe Bury was the daughter of a British army officer, who died in 1864. Her mother was remarried in 1869, to a Canadian civil servant, Herbert O'Meara of Ottawa. O'Meara became accountant and chief clerk in the Department of Militia and Defence in 1881.

proves that my father was not far wrong in stating during the debate on the tariff that although both Mackenzie and Goldwin Smith were free traders there was a wide difference between them for while Mackenzie was a fanatical free trader, Goldwin Smith was a philosophical free trader.

Kindly tell Aunt Louisa that the shaving brush and handkerchiefs came safely to hand. My time will be so much occupied this week between office work and this confounded election[24] that I probably shall not be able to write to her until Monday or Tuesday next. I think we are going to carry the constituency but with the ballot no one can be sure, and I shall feel easier in mind when the result is known.

Yours in haste,
Hugh J. Macdonald

131 To Louisa Macdonald

My dear Louisa   Ottawa Oct. 3, 1880
I have your note & am glad to learn you are well. I fear the Professor is breaking up & I shall advise him to retire and devote himself to literary pursuits. I had a very pleasant trip to England and back but was obliged to work very hard. I have been rewarded by success[25] and am in good health and spirits. I found Agnes *very* well and Mary much improved. Agnes and she will go to New York next month for medical treatment as to Mary's walking. Always my dear Louisa,

most affectionately yours,
John A. Macdonald

132 To James Williamson

My dear Professor   Ottawa Oct. 27, 1880
I send you a copy of the Hansard of last session. You may give them to the College Library – or keep them as you please.

---

[24]In a federal by-election in the riding of Toronto West on August 28, James Beaty, Junior, the Conservative candidate, was elected.
[25]In negotiating a contract for the building of the C.P.R.

I was very sorry I could not go to the College ceremonies but the Pacific Railway forbade.

> Yours always
> John A. Macdonald

133 To Louisa Macdonald

My dear Louisa   *Ottawa Dec. 23, 1880*
The papers arrived all right. I mean the Trust & Loan Cos.
Mrs. Hugh & Daisy arrived this morning all right.
Many merry Christmasses to the Professor & yourself.

> Yours affectionately
> John A. Macdonald

I am pretty well now

134 Louisa Macdonald to James Williamson

My dear Dr Williamson   *Ottawa May 3, [1881]*
Mrs Macpherson[26] would tell you that I have arrived all safe. John is not as well as I had hoped to find him, though not confined to his room he seems weak, and suffers from his liver, and indigestion sometimes (not always). He has pain when he eats, and then he has pain in his right side, a sure indication that his liver is out of order. I have not seen Dr Grant yet although he is here every day and John has every confidence in him, but from Lady Macdonald's description of him Hugh agrees with me in wishing them safely on the other side of the Atlantic where John could get the best advice. Hugh says his father does not want to go, and if Grant were to say to him now, you are too weak, he would give it up. Agnes says there is no doubt he is sincerely interested in every thing about him, but he has a depressing effect on him. He does not encourage him and is always finding out something new, some symptom that may be some new complaint. Do not repeat this to any one as I don't think she would like it, and although she might say more to Mrs Mac if she was

---

[26]Possibly Mrs. James P. Macpherson.

with her Agnes would not like my doing it. I never saw John looking what I would call old till this time. His hair is getting quite grey.

Hugh left this last night. He and his father were busy all yesterday putting things to right. Hugh looked better then [sic] I had hoped for. His little girl comes down this week.

And now for business. I thought I understood you to say that you had paid the full fare when you found you could not renew it, as I did not wish to be tyed [sic] down to the ten days. Now when Hugh looked at my ticket he said it must be renewed and that it can be easily done, so will you let me know exactly what they said. John's secretary Mr. White[27] will have nothing to do but send it to Montreal, so there will be nothing lost. How are they getting on with the house.

Give my love to Maria and Annie.

Ever most faithfully yours
Louisa J. Macdonald

135 HUGH JOHN MACDONALD TO JAMES WILLIAMSON

My dear Mr Williamson   *Toronto May 7, 1881*

I am much obliged to you for your kind expression of sympathy with me in my present trouble. I knew you would feel sorry when you heard the news of poor Jeannie's sudden death,[28] particularly as it took you by surprise. I went down to Ottawa immediately after the funeral and only returned on Tuesday morning. I went back to work at once and think I acted wisely in so doing as the very fact of my thoughts being constantly occupied has had a good effect upon me.

I am at present staying with my brother-in-law Bill Murray and intend to remain with him until Tuesday evening when I hope to be able to send Daisy down to my father's for the summer, and to take possession of my own house again. I have been fortunate enough to secure Hattie, who lived with us for three years, as cook and housekeeper for some months, and as I know by experience that she is honest and economical my mind is easy on the score of the house, particularly as my housemaid

[27]Frederick White was Macdonald's secretary from 1880 to 1883. He was afterwards Comptroller of the North West Mounted Police.
[28]On April 22nd.

has been with me for the last six months & I know she is reliable. Of course I have not as yet formed any plans for the future, but by July I shall have made up my mind what to do and I will then tell you what my plans are.

Meanwhile I remain with love to all,

affectionately yours
Hugh J. Macdonald

136 FROM JAMES WILLIAMSON

My dear Sir John, *Kingston Oct. 13, 1882*

I have a very high opinion of Dr Sullivan,[29] and you will therefore excuse me for what I am now going to say. He has been a faithful and zealous Conservative at all times, and his appointment to one of the vacant Senatorships would be very acceptable to reasonable men of both parties, would promote an able and worthy man, and at the same time still further gratify the Roman Catholics, and secure their loyalty. Kingston is manifestly entitled to one Senatorship at least, and must be represented in the Senate by a man of some ability, if it be at present misrepresented in the House of Commons.[30] I am, with best respects to Lady Macdonald and love to the young ladies,

yours faithfully
Jas. Williamson

137 TO LOUISA MACDONALD

My dear Louisa *Ottawa Dec. 2, 1882*

You must not do anything about the Trust & Loan Company matter. The shareholders in England must fight it out with the Directors.

We are all well here. I am now suffering from a slight attack of

---

[29]Dr. Michael Sullivan (1838-1915) was appointed to the Senate January 29, 1885. He was Professor of Surgery at Queen's.
[30]John A. Macdonald had been defeated in Kingston in the general election of 1878 and in 1882 ran in the riding of Lennox. Alexander Gunn, a Liberal, sat for Kingston, 1882-7.

liver, but a couple of days rest will put me all right. I tell you this as these confounded newspapers may say I am ill. Hugh writes in good spirits.

Alwys yrs affectionately
John A. Macdonald

138 TO JAMES WILLIAMSON

My dear Professor   *Ottawa Jan. 9, 1883*
    Mr. Collins[31] is writing my life I believe for the publishing firm of Hunter Rose & Co. and is I believe a responsible person. What his book may be I don't know, but there can be no harm in Louisa giving you the necessary information to be transmitted to him.
    We are all well here. I have not been very strong but am taking good care of myself for the Session.

Yours always
John A. Macdonald

Love to Louisa

139 TO JAMES WILLIAMSON

My dear Professor   *Ottawa Feb. 19, 1883*
    I am greatly distressed at the indications of a break up in Louisa's case.
    I had heard through James Macpherson that she is not doing well. I greatly fear a fatal issue from these attacks ere long. Hugh will go up in a few days and his impressions will be valuable as he has not seen her for so long a time.
    His intended is with us, an exceedingly nice girl. We are much pleased with her.

Yours sincerely
John A. Macdonald

[31]Joseph Edmund Collins, author of *The Life and Times of the Right Honourable Sir John A. Macdonald* (Toronto, 1883).

My dear Father   Winnipeg May 31, 1883
    McArthur[32] tells me that he wrote to you a day or two about the
suit of Macdonald vs Cunningham in which the Boundary question comes
up and yesterday Ewart[33] mentioned to me that the Ontario Government
were going to support the defendents, who have made up their minds to
carry the case to the Privy Council if the Court of Queen's Bench in
Manitoba decides against them, so it at present looks as if the Boundary
dispute were going to be fought out at last.[34] I presume the Dominion
Government will wish to retain Counsel but of this you are the best judge.
    By the way William [Murdoch] the engineer, stopped me on the
street the other day and asked me to drop you a line about some quarry
in which he is interested and about which he wrote to you some little
time ago. What are his chances of getting it?
    A large number of our friends here are very angry with the course
the "Times" is pursuing and talk of starting another Conservative paper.
Several have asked me if the Dominion government would like to have a
paper here that would advocate their views and I am in rather a quandary
as to what advice to give. I don't think there would be much difficulty in
getting another paper started if you would care about its being done.
Rowe and Farrer between them are making the Times very unpopular[35]
and some of our strongest friends are giving it up and taking the Free
Press.
    We are all well here, thank God, and Daisy is in a great state of
delight because her cat has had kittens. Norquay had a pretty narrow
escape on the address, but as soon as he declared himself a Party man his

[32]J. B. MacArthur, one of Hugh's law partners.

[33]John S. Ewart (1849-1933), a lawyer of very great reputation, practised in Winnipeg, 1872-1904. He was later the author of a number of books and pamphlets
advocating Canadian independence.

[34]Manitoba lost some territory to Ontario when the dispute was settled in 1884.

[35]Amos Rowe was the proprietor, and Edward Farrer the editor, of the Winnipeg
Times. Farrer (1850-1916) had a long journalistic career in Canada and the United
States. A pamphlet which he wrote in 1891 favouring annexation to the United
States was used by John A. Macdonald in his last election of that year to convict
the Liberal Party of "veiled treason".

followers wheeled into line and voted for him like men. He is safe now if he does not intrigue with Greenway & Co.[36]

With love to my mother Mary and the Colonel,

I am yours affectionately
Hugh J. Macdonald

141 TO JAMES WILLIAMSON

My dear Professor   *Ottawa Sept. 11, 1883*

I am distressed to learn that Louisa has been so unwell, and trust she will soon come around. Entre nous I have written Dr. Sullivan about her case today and will I suppose get his answer in a couple of days. We are all well after our two months sojourn at the seaside and must try to remain so.

Yours sincerely
John A. Macdonald

142 TO JAMES WILLIAMSON

My dear Professor   *Ottawa Sept. 18, 1883*

I am greatly distressed about Louisa. Sullivan writes me regularly about her case. I fear she will scarcely be strong enough to come to Ottawa. If I can manage it, I shall run up to Kingston next Saturday but don't say so to her just yet, lest I might be detained. Catherine[37] might get a bed ready for me quietly. I will telegraph before I go so as not to take Louisa by surprise. All well here.

Sincerely yours
John A. Macdonald

143 TO LOUISA MACDONALD

My dear Louisa   *Ottawa Oct. 27, 1883*

I was very glad to receive your letter last night and to receive your own assurance that you feel stronger and better. Still you must be very

---

[36]John Norquay (1841-89) was premier of Manitoba, 1878-87. Thomas Greenway was subsequently premier, 1888-1900.
[37]Catherine Berry, Louisa's maid-companion.

careful and do as Dr. Sullivan bids you. A slight imprudence (in your eyes) might have very serious consequences.

We have bidden Lord Lorne & the Princess good bye and have now Lord Lansdowne to reign in their stead.[38] Lord Lansdowne is a very pleasant man to do business with, and I understand Lady L. is very nice. I have only had one conversation with her yet and cannot speak from personal knowledge.

Agnes & I are now bestowed comfortably at Earnscliffe[39] to remain here until Spring without further travelling.

Agnes is to write you all the news, so I shall only say goodbye.

Yours affectionately
John A. Macdonald

144 TO JAMES WILLIAMSON

My dear Professor   Ottawa Nov. 17, 1883
    I send you a book of yours. I don't know how it got among mine.
    The cheap editions of the 3 reviews, Fortnightly, Contemporary & 19th Century are no longer issued.

Yours sincerely
John A. Macdonald

145 TO JAMES WILLIAMSON

My dear Professor   Ottawa Nov. 21, 1883
    On enquiry I find that no local Examiner is required at Kingston. I shall however bear Mr. Givins in mind should one be needed at any time. I am glad to hear such good accounts of Louisa.
    We are all well here and slowly getting our house in order.

Yours sincerely
John A. Macdonald

[38] As Governor General.
[39] Macdonald bought Earnscliffe in January 1883, but did not move in until October.

My dear Sir John,   *Kingston Nov. 26, 1883*
    Some of his friends have asked Principal Grant[40] and myself to speak
to you about my old student Mr. James McLennan Q.C. in connection
with the vacant judgeship. You know how unwilling I am to speak to
you about any thing of the sort great, or small, and I am no lawyer. I can
say this, however, that in his studies *in my office* he was highly distinguished by his sound and clear judgment and his general literary culture. His appointment would be exceedingly agreeable to the Authorities
of Queen's, he having been for a number of years one of its Trustees.
I understand that some of the leading Conservative lawyers in Toronto
are interesting themselves in his favour.
    Louisa is still keeping pretty well, and has been out twice or thrice
for a short walk. I am always,

yours faithfully
Jas. Williamson

147 TO JAMES WILLIAMSON

My dear Professor   *Ottawa Nov. 28, 1883*
    Before receiving your note about James McLennan the vacancy on
the Bench had been filled up by the appt of Mr. Rose of Toronto.[41]
    We are all well here and glad to hear of Louisa's improvement.

Sincerely yours
John A. Macdonald

148 TO JAMES WILLIAMSON

My dear Professor   *Ottawa Jan. 28, 1884*
    The St. James Gazette is now coming to me again. I shall send you the
back numbers as the leading articles are always interesting altho' the

---

[40]George Monro Grant, Principal of Queen's, 1877-1902.
[41]John Edward Rose, a Toronto lawyer, was appointed to the Supreme Court of
Ontario, December 4, 1883.

news may be old. I am sorry that the Canadian Illustrated News is defunct. So that I can no longer send it to Louisa. Give her my love & let me know how she is getting on.

Yours always
John A. Macdonald

149 TO JAMES WILLIAMSON

My dear Professor   *Ottawa June 20, 1884*
    Pardon me for stealing your Hat. I owe you a new one. Get one from Clark Wright or anywhere else & charge it to me.
    Will you kindly send me the Bismuth prescription.
    My address is St. Patrick P.Q. We hope to get off tomorrow. Love to Louisa,

yours etc.
John A. Macdonald

150 FROM HUGH JOHN MACDONALD

My dear Father   *Winnipeg July 8, 1884*
    I have yours of the 2nd and have written to Mr Wood stating that you know General Butler so slightly that you can not take the liberty of giving a letter of introduction to him. From what I have heard of him I should think he would not hesitate to make any use of such a letter that would suit his purpose and at the present moment he might find it to his advantage to pose as the friend of the Prime Minister of Canada. What do you think of his chances as a candidate for the Presidency?[42]
    I am quite at a loss to know where your letter is written from. I thought you were going to Riviere du Loup for the Summer but you appear to have gone elsewhere. Please let me know what your address is.

[42]General Benjamin F. Butler of Massachusetts ran for president in the election of November 1884, as the candidate of the National Greenback Labour Party. He ran a very poor third. Mr. Wood was presumably some sort of political aide to Butler.

Col Houghton[43] is getting on fairly well as Deputy-Adjutant-General. He does not go on sprees, and I have never seen him under the influence of liquor though I think that day in and day out he drinks more than is good for him. I hardly know how to answer your question as to whether he gives one the impression that he is a good officer as I have had no opportunity of judging of his ability as a military man. Speaking, however, from what I have seen of the man, I should say that he had plenty of pluck and determination and would make a capital *fighting officer*, but I must frankly admit I do not think he would be a capable commander, for he has not much head and still less judgment. I don't know whether he is a good drill or not, but have no doubt he is good enough to fill the position he occupies.

The volunteer force is small, consisting of one troop of cavalry, one Battery of Artillery and the 90th Battalion. The troop of cavalry like nearly all volunteer cavalry is far from efficient, and in case of trouble would only be good for outpost duty. The men in most cases do not owned [*sic*] the horses they ride and neither men nor horses are well drilled. The Artillery is up to its full strength and well disciplined for a Militia Battery. The 90th had at the inspection which took place a week or two ago, 262 men on parade. It has been so recently formed that it is hard to tell how it will turn out, but it is very well officered and the men are all picked men and it is at the present time much better drilled than most country Battalions in Ontario. I think there is every occasion to hope that in time it will be to this Province what the Queen's Own are to Ontario and the Vics are to Quebec. All the Winnipeg corps can be depended upon in case of the Farmers Union kicking up a row, as the townspeople have no sympathy with this movement,[44] and if any trouble of this sort arose there would be no difficulty in raising another Battalion

[43]Colonel Charles Frederick Houghton (1839-98), a former captain in the British army, was M.P. for Yale, B.C., 1871-2, and Deputy Adjutant General of Militia, of B.C., 1873-81, of Manitoba, 1881-8, and of Quebec, 1888-96.

[44]The Farmer's Protective Union of Manitoba was formed in 1883. The union complained of such matters as low wheat prices, high machinery prices, high freight rates, high tariffs, railway and elevator monopolies, land speculation, and federal control of public lands in Manitoba. The movement lost much of the popular support it initially enjoyed as a result of its convention held in Winnipeg in March 1884, at which one of the union leaders recommended that Manitoba secede from Canada if grievances were not quickly redressed.

providing Osborne Smith, Jim McLeod, S. L. Bedson, Hayter Reed[45] or any other man well known to the people as an officer were commissioned to raise it. I hope however there will be no necessity for a display of force and I very much doubt whether even the most discontented of the farmers would venture to appeal to arms.

The Militia arms and stores, including ammunition were until quite recently perfectly unprotected, the arms of the 90th being stored in a skating rink and the powder rifles and other military stores being in a couple of frame huts in what is called Fort Osborne. Within the last few days Kennedy[46] has put a guard on the skating rink but the arms and supplies in Fort Osborne are still unprotected. Ten Mounted Police are quartered in the Fort it is true, but as far as I can see or hear they have not been in the habit of taking charge of the Militia stores, and when passing the Fort, as I frequently do I have never seen even a sentry on duty. If you think there is any chance of trouble this ought to be attended to at once, as it would never do to let the Union open the campaign by capturing all the arms in the country.

Gertie and Dee are both well and join me in love to you, my mother Mary and the Colonel.

Affectionately yours
Hugh J. Macdonald

151 TO JAMES WILLIAMSON

My dear Professor   *Riviere du Loup Aug. 14, 1884*
I was not altogether unprepared for your letter. Annie had informed me that Louisa did not improve from her stay at Orchard Beach and Joanna wrote me that she was distressed by the change in Louisa's appearance.

---

[45]Lieutenant-Colonel William Osborne Smith, of Winnipeg, Deputy Adjutant General of Militia in Manitoba, 1871-81. James Farquharson Macleod (1836-94) became Commissioner of the North West Mounted Police in 1877 and a Puisne Judge of the Supreme Court of the Northwest Territories, 1887. S. L. Bedson was Warden of Stoney Mountain Penitentiary. Hayter Reed, at this time Assistant Indian Commissioner and a member of the Northwest Council, was Deputy Superintendent General of Indian Affairs, 1893-7.
[46]Lieutenant-Colonel William Nassau Kennedy, officer commanding the 90th Winnipeg Battalion of Rifles, and also Registrar of the County of Selkirk.

We must now I fear give up hope of her restoration to health and try to make her as comfortable as possible while she lingers with us. I know that she will have in you all that care and kindness can give her. I shall be obliged by your writing me from time to time how the poor dear is doing.

We are enjoying fine weather here, and shall stay until about 8th Sept. unless I am summoned by business to Ottawa at an earlier day. Agnes & Mary are both doing well.

Always yours sincerely
John A. Macdonald

152 FROM JAMES WILLIAMSON

My dear Sir John,   Kingston Aug. 25, 1884
I am glad to say that Louisa is better. The warm weather which we have had since I wrote seems to agree with her, so that she has been able to drive up and see Mrs Macpherson, and go over last Saturday with Mrs. Sullivan and Catherine in the boat to Cape Vincent.

I sent you some time ago a mixture such as I had got made up for me at Hobarts, but not remembering the exact prescription I wrote home for it as I have found it better than any other. I have now got it and send it as follows,

"Stomach Powder
1 oz rhubarb, 1 oz bicarbonate of soda, and ½ oz bismuth.
To be mixed together, and a small quantity (as much as would lie on a sixpence) to be taken a quarter of an hour before food."

This is the prescription of the best Edinburgh physicians, and I have found it an excellent one. The mixture I sent you before was good but not quite up to the mark, not the genuine thing, and not in a word the Simon pure, and may be thrown out, and the other ordered in its place.

I am always my dear Sir John,

Yours faithfully
Jas. Williamson

Kindest remembrance to Lady Macdonald and my dear Miss Macdonald

153 To James Williamson

My dear Professor   *Ottawa Dec. 24, 1884*

Thanks for yours of the 22nd. I need not say that the Oatcake and Sheepsheads will be most acceptable.

Please to tell Mrs. Allen[47] that when Mr. Kirkpatrick[48] next comes to Ottawa, we will act together and endeavour to obtain the lease she wants.

Give my love to Louisa and say that I shall try to run up some Saturday night soon, and stay over Sunday with her. I shall telegraph when I can get away.

The demonstration at Toronto was really a magnificent one and has struck terror into the Grits.

Wishing you & Louisa many happy returns of the season. Believe me,

yours affectionately
John A. Macdonald

154 From Hugh John Macdonald

My dear Father   *Fish Creek Apr. 26, 1885*

As there is a mail going out tonight I drop you a line to let you know that we have had a rather hot engagement[49] with the rebels and that I am allright. We found the enemy about 9:30 A.M. on Friday in one of the strongest natural positions I ever saw and had a serious engagement for about 4 hours. We drove them back and out of the field on both flanks but failed to dislodge them from a very strongly fortified position in the centre which was situated in a deep and thickly wooded gulch or ravine from which they fired with great effect. The only way to get them out was by bayonet charge and this the General would not allow, though Col. Houghton, Capt. Wise[50] and I offered to lead the men. Unfortunately Lord Melgund[51] was on the other side of the river with the 10th Royals

---

[47]Probably Mrs. M. J. Allen of Kingston, a widow.
[48]Sir George Airey Kirkpatrick (1841-99) was M.P. for Frontenac from 1870 until his appointment as Lieutenant-Governor of Ontario in 1892.
[49]The battle of Fish Creek, which took place on April 24. Hugh was a lieutenant with the 90th Winnipeg Rifles.
[50]Captain Henry Ellison Wise was acting as aide-de-camp to Major-General Frederick Middleton, the commander-in-chief of the Canadian forces.
[51]Middleton's chief-of-staff.

and Winnipeg Battery. Had he been on hand the charge would have been made and our losses would have been much smaller. At this present moment the total loss is 9 killed & 43 wounded many mortally but the men are in good spirits & quite ready for another fight. I fought in the front rank of skirmishers on the right but did not receive a scratch though men were hit all round me and I was a good deal exposed during a series of rushes by which we carried their position on the right. I was pleased and rather surprised to find that I was quite cool under fire and perfectly able to handle my men. The rebels withdrew from their stronghold as soon as darkness set in and have gone we know not where though we presume they have fallen back to Batoche Crossing where I presume we shall follow them tomorrow.

Please excuse me for writing on such paper[52] and in pencil as if I dont use what I have at hand I should not be able to write at all

With love to my mother and Mary, I remain,

affectionately yours
Hugh J. Macdonald

155 TO LOUISA MACDONALD

My dear Louisa   *Earnscliffe May 9, 1885*
I send you a pencil note from poor Hugh which perhaps you may be able to make out. So far he has – thank God! escaped & done himself no discredit by his conduct in the field. I am holding out pretty well in the hard fight we have here. Love to the Professor,

yours affectionately
John A. Macdonald

156 TO JAMES WILLIAMSON

My dear Professor   *Ottawa Sept. 28, 1885*
I have had a letter from Judge Gowan.[53] He does not like to have his gift of the $500 of his Parliamentary allowance to be dignified by the name of the Gowan Bursary.

[52]A page torn from a small notebook.
[53]Sir James Robert Gowan (1815-1909) was county court judge of Simcoe County, Ontario, for forty years, 1843-83. In 1885 he was appointed to the Senate.

He is however giving another sum of $400 to the College through Principal Grant. I think he would like that to be invested for a Gowan Scholarship.

Yours always
John A. Macdonald

157 FROM MARY MACDONALD

My dear old Father,   *Ottawa Dec. 22, 1885*

Forgive me for not having written to you before I know I have been very neglectful but I could not help it. I received your card this morning and thought it was lovely.

I suppose you will soon be thinking of coming home,[54] I hope so for I miss you very much, but of course as it is going to do you good I must not grumble. We had a lovely trip after we left you we were down at Halifax and St John. I saw Ada and Colonel Montmorency,[55] I suppose she thinks him all perfection as you do Mamma. Mamma is away just now and how long she is going to stay I do not know. I hope you will bring me the ring I asked you for. How are Mr and Mrs Stephen?[56] I suppose you see them a good deal. Have you seen Her Majesty the Queen? Do you remember what you told me last year about kissing her hand?

It is very cold here now. I suppose it is not so cold in England. What are you going to do on Christmas day? I will miss you very much. I suppose you will be out in time for your birthday, and then wont we hug and kiss each other. Were you very sick crossing?

And now dear Papa as I have told you all the news I can think off [sic] I must say good bye, hoping that if you do not sail soon after this letter you will let me have one in return.

Believe me my dear Papa with love and many kisses for your dear old self,

your affectionate child
Mary

P.S.   If Mamma does not come home for Christmas I am going out with Mrs Oswald to spend the day at her mothers.

[54]Macdonald was in England for a short holiday.
[55]Ada Bury (see above, p. 142) married Lieutenant-Colonel Raymond Oliver de Montmorency, of the Royal Irish Rifles, in April 1885. Colonel Montmorency and his battalion were stationed at Halifax.
[56]George Stephen (afterwards Lord Mount Stephen), president of the C.P.R.

PART FOUR ❦ 1886-1891

For thirty years he had been offering, or threatening, to retire as party leader, but he stayed on – partly because there was nothing else he wanted to do, partly because there was always someone or some circumstance to convince him that he was indispensable, partly because there was no one whom he really wanted to be his political heir. "Langevin is the only possible successor," he confided to Sir Leonard Tilley. Perhaps. But the thought of Sir Hector as prime minister did not give him much comfort. "Langevin has aged very much," he wrote to Sir Charles Tupper a few months later, "and is inert and useless except in office." Yet there was no one else. He complained that his ministry was too old, but he was somehow unwilling or unable to attract fresh new faces. There was Thompson, whom he had recruited from the Nova Scotia bench to be Minister of Justice, but Thompson's health was dubious and he had an even more serious drawback which made him unsuitable. Like Langevin he was a Roman Catholic, and in the eyes of many of Macdonald's fellow English Canadians both were something worse – Langevin, a French Canadian, and Thompson, to use the quaint nineteenth-century term, a "pervert", who had forsaken his original Methodist faith. For the bad old days of bitter racial feeling had returned to plague Macdonald in his old age. At a time when he might have hoped for a serene political twilight he found himself working harder than ever, found his path more hazardous and difficult, found himself fighting with all his remaining strength to preserve his vision of the Dominion that should be, and to preserve his political skin. Was it his own doing? Certainly as he grew older he became less flexible, less patient with dissent, less able to distinguish between matters that had to be dealt with and matters that could be

159

postponed. But this hardening of mental arteries was more than offset by an innate political sure-footedness, a lifetime of experience, and a knowledge of men and affairs possessed by no other politician, then or since. The national malaise, and Macdonald's share in it, stemmed from deeper currents in Canadian life, currents of race hatred stirred by a single agonizing event – the hanging of Louis Riel, a man who, in the irreconcilable views of English and French Canadians, was either a traitor to the British crown or a martyr to Anglo-Saxon imperialism. Riel had led an armed rebellion against the government of Canada. He had been convicted of treason and executed for his crime. But, and here the affair touched Macdonald very closely, did it all have to have happened at all?

John A. Macdonald was a tolerant man, judged by the standards of his contemporaries, perhaps an exceptionally tolerant man. From an early stage in his career he had devoted his energies to Canadian unity, to promoting mutual respect and co-operation between French and English, Protestant and Catholic. There was, in the words of his secretary and biographer, Joseph Pope, "an entire absence of prejudice in his large and liberal mind". He was nonetheless a man of his day, who shared the instincts and assumptions of his times and of his contemporaries. Deeper in his being than any conscious rejection of bigotry lay an inborn, unbidden, unquestioning assumption of the inherent superiority of all things British, and the consequent inferiority, in however small degree, of every other living human being. He was not, to add an additional phrase of Pope's, "blind to the defects of the French character". It was this incipient, elemental racism that got in his way in dealing with the agitation in the Northwest, which caused him to misunderstand and underestimate the national impulses of both the Métis and the French Canadians of Quebec. He simply could not take the Métis seriously. To him they were a small degenerate group of half-breeds who, whatever they were given, would either "drink it or waste it or sell it".[1] Nor could he take seriously enough the French-Canadian reaction to the conviction and execution of Riel. It was only their excitable Latin way. "The French-Canadians, with the usual furia franchese",[2] had temporarily taken up Riel's cause.

Almost certainly, if he had been less indifferent to the grievances of the people of the Northwest, Macdonald could have prevented the rebellion from happening. Could he also have prevented the political and

[1]Canada, House of Commons Debates, 1885, Vol. IV, p. 3118.
[2]Minto Papers, M.G. 27, II B1. Macdonald to Viscount Melgund, September 1, 1886.

racial storm that followed the execution of Riel by having his death sentence commuted? To many people Riel was simply insane and his life could therefore be spared. Was Macdonald's decision to allow Riel to hang (as has often been alleged) taken on political grounds? He was, even despite himself, a politician. Yet there is not the slightest doubt that he genuinely believed that Riel was guilty, and sane. Whatever lay behind his decision the consequences were the same. In purely political terms the hanging of Riel may well have been the greatest blunder of his life.

It was not long before he discovered how potent the furia franchese could be. In January 1887, it swept the provincial Conservative administration in Quebec out of office, and the following month a federal election called by Macdonald on short notice produced further dramatic changes among French-Canadian voters. The Conservative majority in the province, which had stood at thirty-one, was reduced to one. Four years later, in the general election of 1891, the majority of one became a minority of five. It would be sixty-seven years and seventeen more general elections before the Conservative Party would again win the greatest number of seats in the Province of Quebec. The French-Canadian bloc of votes on which the party had for so many years relied for its foundation could no longer be depended upon. The alliance of French and English, forged with Macdonald's active assistance in the Liberal-Conservative coalition of 1854, had abruptly come unstuck.

Macdonald's last political years were marked by gradual but unmistakable retreat. Each election eroded his parliamentary majority a little further. The provincial governments, almost all in the hands of hostile political forces, asserted ever more boldly their "provincial rights" and chipped away at the edifice of central power that Macdonald had been at such pains to construct. In retreat or not, he went on, following more or less by instinct well-worn political paths. He fought his last election on historic, familiar ground, offering Canadians the choice of loyalty to British institutions or the horrible alternative, the dread spectre of American annexation. As a young man he had fought his first election on the same issue, the same choice – American mob rule or British monarchy. The words he had used then, the words he had used in another loyalty election in 1861, were appropriate and potent still. "Let there be no looking to Washington . . . but let the cry, with the moderate party, be Canada united . . . under one Sovereign."

He said and probably meant that 1891 would be his last election. "I intend to sing my nunc dimittis if the election makes the country safe," he told a supporter. Perhaps, if his last illness had not made it an academic question, he would have resigned. He was old and tired. He did not expect to live a great deal longer. In private as well as political ways he began to prepare for the inevitable. On September 4, 1890, he signed the last of a series of wills disposing of his property. Agnes and Mary were already provided for by the trust fund set up by his friends in 1872, but he wanted to make sure that his wife and his daughter, "who will probably be through life incapable of managing her own affairs", would be able to stay in Earnscliffe as long as they wished and that such additional assets as he had acquired, including some C.P.R. capital stock, should be used for their benefit. The last provision of his will concerned the disposition of his body. "I desire that I shall be buried in the Kingston Cemetery near the grave of my mother as I promised her that I should be there buried." His wish was carried out all too soon. His health which had seemed so miraculously preserved had in reality been dangerously fragile for a long time, too fragile to withstand the strain of a winter election. On June 11, 1891, his body was placed beside that of his mother, near to the bodies of his sisters, his father, his first wife, and his first son.

"The life of Sir John Macdonald," his opponent Wilfrid Laurier said at his death, "is the history of Canada." Canada was his creation, and he had never ceased to labour for the nation he had brought into being, even if it would never quite become the nation he wished it to be. All politicians, and Sir John A. Macdonald was no exception, are cordially hated by large numbers of their countrymen, yet surely no Canadian politician was ever more widely and genuinely beloved, more deeply and sincerely mourned. Canada would go on without this human, humorous, tolerant, profoundly wise old man. But Canada would never be the same.

My dear Aunt Lou   *Earnscliffe Jan. 19, 1886*

Sir John arrived today looking well & shiny & in excellent spirits. He had a nice little reception, made a nice little speech and drove home very contentedly after all the gay doings in London town. He had had a cold before leaving, but the voyage which he says was a very good one seems to have done him good. He had a beautiful cabin in the *Oregon*, & the Stephens & Donald Smiths[1] were with him – all good company. He was so tired and worried when he went away that it quite inspirits me to see him so cheery.

I hope you are feeling well, but the suddeness [sic] of this cold weather is trying to all. Oswalt tells me some days during my absence were colder than almost any she ever felt in Ottawa before.

It was very cold in Regina where I was at the time, but not colder I think than at Ottawa tho' the glass was several degrees lower. I saw Hugh & Gertie at their cozy and pretty home in Winnipeg & brought dear little Dee home with me. She is grown but looks thin, still she seems very bright & strong, with a good appetite & sleep. She is one of the gentlest sweetest children I ever saw, so easily managed. She is devoted to Gerty & Gerty to her. "Jack" is a fine boy, like both parents, especially Gertie about the eyes. But you will soon see them all for yourself for Hugh promises to bring them all down very soon, to come here first & then in Kingston & then Toronto, but of course he has written to you.

I have been roaming in Sir John's absence & Mary has had two months complete holiday doing exactly what she liked, no massage, no movements but friends & fun & idling. On the 11th she gave a little Ball in honor of her father's birthday & had over 80 guests. No children this time as she is so nearly 17! I arranged all her plans before I left for the North West, sent out all the invitations & asked two ladies to help Mary receive, & Norah & Oswalt managed the rest.

As for me I have been to the summit of the Canadian Rocky Mountains by C.P.R.! To Mount Stephen this side of the Pacific slope & Kicking Horse Pass. It was by far the most interesting & delightful trip I ever made in my life. I asked Judge & Mrs Brooks[2] to go as my guests & took a butler & a maid & we had besides the car porter who is also cook. At

[1]Donald Smith (1820-1914), afterwards Lord Strathcona.
[2]Edward Towle Brooks of Sherbrooke, Quebec, M.P. for Sherbrooke from 1872 until 1882, when he was appointed to the Superior Court of Quebec.

Regina the Governor & Mrs Dewdney[3] joined us & went to the Rockies with me & remained at Regina when we left. We started off quietly, very few had any idea I was going away at all.

No one can form an idea of what that country is (even in Winter) without seeing it. The wonder of the Prairies, the marvel of the long long distances the exquisite beauty of the mountains, the wild scenery of Lake Superior & the wonderful management of an railway 2500 miles long, all requires to be seen to be believed in!

We were absent 16 days and nights, spent 2 days & 2 nights at Winnipeg, two days & a night at Regina, two nights at Canmore (in the mountains) & half a day & night at Port Arthur & travelled all the rest. Every day was a pleasure & a new interest but it must wait till I see you to be told of. The cold was severe, but not any more so, so far as I could tell, than at Ottawa or Quebec. We had only one snow storm & blizzard at night & next morning the snow must have been blown away for there was very little in the prairie anywhere. The weather (for the most part) was brilliantly fine and clear.

West of Heron Bay which is on *this* side of Lake Superior there was very little snow hardly anywhere & at Calgary & little in the Rockies. We had a special from Calgary to the summit & back to Regina & as the road from Calgary had not been travelled by cars for 3 weeks & as we were not delayed for 5 minutes, you may fancy the track was clear.

We visited the wonderful Banff Springs & the gas well at Cassils, two coal mines & a waterfall & did & saw no end of new & delightful things. The scenery at Calgary is very lovely, prairies undulating in soft swelling folds covered with natural hay, for it really is hay, then the rounded foothills widening & stretching into the snow capped mountain peaks that rise into the blue sky, too beautiful for words. I travelled in the car platform or on the engine of the specials & was more than delighted with all I saw.

The C.P.R. were ever so good to me. Mr Van Horne[4] said I might go where I liked. Superintendents had a sort of charge of us & joined our party in their own cars. Altogether it was too delightful.

What astonished me was the comfort & ease of the railway, its

---

[3]The Honourable Edgar Dewdney (1835-1916), M.P. for Yale, British Columbia, 1872-8, Lieutenant-Governor of the Northwest Territories, 1881-8, Minister of the Interior, 1888-92, Lieutenant-Governor of British Columbia, 1892-7.
[4]Sir William Cornelius Van Horne (1843-1915), at this time general manager and later president of the C.P.R.

strict punctuality, its quiet & prompt management & its little motion. We read, played games, wrote letters, all generally with great ease & this on a line far away in an almost uninhabited country & in depth of a Canadian winter.

The scenery on Lake Superior is the wildest I ever saw. They gave me a special so that I could see it by daylight. The rock cuttings, & trestle bridges spanning immense valleys indeed bridging mountains together, are wonderful to see. As for the Prairies they seem ready prepared farms, no trees to root out no stones to pick up no need of fences, beautiful fertile land stretching away limitless to the clear horizon. I thought the sunrise & sunset on prairies beautiful till I saw them among the rockies – there they delighted my eyes.

We had no mishaps & only a few hours detention near Heron Bay about 580 miles from Ottawa but we met the friends punctually at 7:30 Friday night last. When I had invited them I was 1600 miles away.

Ottawa seems so dull & tame & stupid & old after that new wonderful western world with its breadth & length & clear air & wonderfully exhilarating atmosphere that always seems to lure me on!

We lost 3 hours in our time. West of Canmore my clock at 10 A.M. was 7 A.M. Pacific Standard Time! The 1st change is at Port Arthur the second at Brandon, 3d at Canmore. We were only 500 miles from the Pacific but I had to hurry homeward to meet Sir John.

I had previously as you know taken Mary to Halifax St John Dalhousie & Fredericton – so that makes nearly 7000 miles travelling in the Jamaica since Nov. 21, the day Sir John sailed. Sir John is quite pleased with my visit to the West & shall never rest till he goes too!

I also spent a week at Sherbrooke with Judge & Mrs Brooks. I found Mary looking & seeming particularly well. Her father is pleased to see her looking so much better than she was early in winter. Hewitt writes me he is being fairly well & comfortable at Dansville.[5] Best love to Aunt Maria, Annie & Joanna. As I have not time to write to them yet will you kindly send on this letter for them to read as Aunt Maria may like to hear about my trip. It has done me ever so much good. I feel a new person. Constantly nursing the sick & housekeeping in Ottawa for a large household & looking after all sorts of things daily almost for 2 years is fatiguing!

Alas! My excellent Norah, cook & acting housekeeper is going to be

---

[5]Hewitt Bernard had become, and was to remain, more or less of an invalid. He was in a large private sanitorium in Dansville, New York.

married *at once*. I am broken hearted utterly, but she is such a dear soul I cannot be selfish & can only be glad she will be so happily settled after *ten* years betrothal!

Good night dear Aunt Lou. Please ask Dr. Williamson when he is coming to see us & believe me,

yours very affectionately
Agnes Macdonald

Sir John is sound asleep or he would send a lot of love. He will write tomorrow or next day & give an account of himself—

A.M.

159 TO LOUISA MACDONALD

My dear Louisa   *Earnscliffe Jan.* 21, 1886
    I have received the Trust & Loan cheque and papers. I send you a cheque for $50 being

for interest on loan of $1000	35.00
New Years Gift	15.00
	$50.00

    Annie & Johnnie both write about your health or rather want of health. Make the Professor write me all about you.

Yours affectionately
John A. Macdonald

160 FROM JAMES WILLIAMSON

My dear Sir John,   *Kingston Jan.* 28, 1886
    Alexander Macpherson is willing and his friends are anxious for him to return to Kingston if he could get something to do here. It is reported that Macalister of the Customs House is about to be superannuated. If so I am sure no one would be better fitted to fill his situation than Alexander, a worthy first rate man of business, and universally respected. Excuse me

writing now about this, but I know it would be a good thing for one who would most faithfully and ably discharge the duties of the post, and whom the failure of the Montreal Banks has left poorly off. I am glad to say Louisa is still somewhat better.

I am, yours faithfully
Jas. Williamson

161 Agnes Macdonald to James Williamson

My dear Dr Williamson   *Earnscliffe Feb. 4,* [1886]
    I was so very stupid in telling you that the journey from Winnipeg to Ottawa occupied 84 hours instead of 60 that I must write a few lines of apology & explanation!
    In our case we remained over at *Port Arthur* for a night & half a day, so as to make the trip round Lake Superior by daylight & then waited at Heron Bay till the next days train came up, thus arriving in Ottawa on Friday instead of Thursday morning. Had we come straight thro' leaving Winnipeg at 6:30 P.M. on Monday we should have arrived here about the same hour A.M. on Thursday! but we lost a whole train by our delay in Port Arthur.
    I remembered this just after you left today & hasten to explain my stupid error!
    Hugh & Gertrude leaving Winnipeg last Monday were due here this morning Thursday, but they are late & will not arrive till 7 P.M. tonight, near 12 hours late. It is due to the severe weather. I have just returned from the station where I went to enquire.
    I hope you had a nice journey & found Aunt Lou pretty well. With much love,

yrs affectionately
Agnes Macdonald

We hope *very* much you will come soon again. You will be heartily welcome it gives us great pleasure to see you & next time you must stay with us all the time & not go to your friends all the time. I did not thank you for giving Mary such a lovely ring, it was too kind of you, she wears it with much pride.

My dear Sir John,   *Kingston Feb. 8, 1886*

Mr Kirkpatrick is to write you about Alexr. Macpherson for the appointment of Inspector of Weights and Measures. Alexr. is a Kingstonian and will reside here as before, and no one would do the duty more faithfully, or be more generally respected by all classes. You have only to intimate in the way you know best your opinion on the subject and that of Mr Kirkpatrick, and the thing is done, and may I add, the sooner the better, for it will be a good deed, and greatly for the public interest. It is therefore and because of my great esteem for Alexander that I now write you o᾿ the subject. I am with kindest remembrances to Lady Macdonald & love to Mary,

yours always

Jas. Williamson

P.S. Louisa has all ready here for Hugh & Mrs Macdonald and bairns and sends her love. We long to see them all.

163 FROM MARY MACDONALD

My dearest Papa   *Banff Station April 6, 1887*

As we have got to the end of our journey, I thought I would write & tell you. Here we are surrounded on all sides by snow clapped mountains & four or five small log houses. We were very glad to get your telegram yesterday, saying you were quite well & also that you had received our letters.

We enjoyed our short stay at Winnipeg very much, Edith, Oswalt & I went to Government House, the others slept in the car, & came for their meals. When we arrived it was a lovely day, but towards evening it began to blow & to snow, & Sunday was simply a frightful day, a strong North West wind blowing a regular Blizzard, but when we left on Monday, there was hardly any trace of the storm left. At Brandon we saw such a lot of people at the station, among whom was an Indian. As we went pass [sic] Oak Lake and Hargrave we saw quite a number, on the west side of the South Saskatchewan, we saw several Indian Tepees.

Are you very lonely without us, do you miss our evening talk? You are ever in my thoughts. Mother & Miss McLimont are ready to start for the Springs to see what our accomadations [sic] are like.[6] And now dear Papa, I think I had better conclude Mother sends her dearest love, & says she thinks she had better stay a few days to settle us, so with very best love & kisses, ever dearest Papa,

your loving daughter
Mary

164 AGNES MACDONALD TO LOUISA MACDONALD

Dear Auntie Lou   *Earnscliffe* [May] 21, [1887]
    Thanks for your letter. I am writing you again, because I have so much to do for the next few weeks (D.V.) that I do not know when I may have time later. I have just finished a long story to dear Mary, from whom I hear constantly.
    She is very well & happy & I hear most comfortable accounts of her improvement. Mrs Dewdney who was at Banff a week or so ago wrote me a charming letter saying she was struck with her great improvement. Especially she dwelt on Mary's face being so healthy & smiling. She was using her right hand to do her felt work. They were very comfortable & cozy. As for the snow there were 2 storms when I was there. It is not the least like *our* snow storms.
    The mountain tops seem to attract snow flurries that whirl round them in bright sunlight & then come down into the valley while sun is still shining & after half an hour all is bright again. The air is so dry there is no rawness at all.
    I am sending up a large tent for her to sit in, during the day & by this time I have no doubt the weather is lovely in that sweet place. I am thankful she is there & not here during this session for the house is always full & busy. I have tried to teach Mary what my mother tried to teach me, that she must do, or have done, what was best for her & for others & not grumble, & she has perfect faith in our plans for her. I shall always try to get her away for the session for she does not do well here unless she can be with me & have all her quiet comforts as usual. This is impossible during the session.

[6]A log cottage built by the C.P.R. at Banff, overlooking the Bow River, had been given to the Macdonalds as a summer retreat. The cottage still stands, close to the Banff Springs Hotel.

The Professor has chosen a nice time for going to Winnipeg. How pleased the Hugh's will be to see him! I do *hope* he will go to Victoria. He ought to! It is a nice trip. For yourself I am quite sure you would find the journey, even to Winnipeg very fatiguing. 60 hours of constant travelling is fatiguing to anyone, comfortable as the C.P.R. trains are, you have no idea how tired you would be. The stoppages are so short, the movement so constant that it would try your strength sadly I fear. Used as I am to railway travelling I always feel my head & brain weary & shaken for days after a long journey.

Hewitt is in very nice lodgings in town. He requires two large rooms adjoining on a ground floor, which if we gave him here at Earnscliffe would reduce us to *one* room. He requires special hours, special meals, special quiet & special care. He does not like to meet more than one or two people a day & is so unselfish & so sensible that he would not on any account, add these arrangements to an already busy household in Sir John's house.

Earnscliffe is looking *very* pretty. The Colonel comes down daily, or drives with me. He generally drives with friends in the morning, sees people from 12 to 1, dines, rests & comes here at 3 till about 8, that is unless we have a large party, when I go & drive out with him early.

I am very much taken up with my garden & expect a lot of flowers to put out today, besides those I have. It is a large place & more costly than I like. So far I have a fair laborer for $1 a day but he knows nothing of gardening. The trees are very pretty here, & my vines growing fast. It is really green & pretty in July when we generally go away. The house wants painting & papering too, which I am greatly dreading. I want it done in August but do not know if there will be time. I am waiting for the painting & papering before I recover my very shabby chairs & renew my shabby curtains. In the meantime I am trying to make the outside look pretty! I had 16 to lunch on Thursday & we have 20 to dine today after my reception.

My cook is improving but I have to see after everything or it goes awry, but she is so good tempered & useful I like her much, so far as she goes.

I *hope* Sir J. will go to England. Perhaps I may go too, but I don't much care about it. Sir John always greatly benefits by the change & voyage. I never saw anyone improve by a voyage as he does. I am thankful to say there is no real occasion for a voyage this year, only he has business & the change is useful.

I never saw him so well at this time of the session as he is now. The Tilley's left us after a weeks visit yesterday. It was so delightful to have them! such dear old friends. I expect Emma Aikens[7] today for a fortnight or so.

By & by I am going to fish in the Restigouche about the 20th with the Brooks & Mr Leckie – Mrs. Leckie[8] will remain at Parrsboro with the new baby. The fishing time is my holiday. It sets me up. I love the camping & the quiet of those green woods far away from everybody. Sir J. has not yet decided if he will go to England. You may be sure he will *never* take a peerage! It would make us both ridiculous & tho' we have been both very wicked often, I humbly think we have never been ridiculous! Nothing would distress me more than to see him – that most unfortunate of men – a *very poor Lord*. In no way possible could we live as nobles ought & are expected to do & for my part I do not think Sir John would be made a whit greater than he is if he was a Duke tomorrow with £70,000 a year!

I know his mind well on the subject and am *positively certain* that he would never make so great a mistake as to be a peer! The very rumour is hurtful because people may imagine he would like it if it was offered! I hope dear Aunt Maria is better. Joan wrote to tell me of all your fine plans for the reception of the guards. I mean the fine plan of the "Ladies of Kingston". I hope the day will be fine. Joan wanted me to go up but of course I couldnt!

Now it is 7-30 & Alphonse has breakfasted & I must go into the fowl yard & garden. The grass watered all night is lovely in the sunlight.

With love to Dr. Williamson,

yrs affectionately
A. Macdonald

I hope Celia[9] is better.

---

[7]Emma Frances Aikins, daughter of the Honourable James Cox Aikins, Secretary of State 1867-73, 1878-80, Minister of Inland Revenue, 1880-2, Lieutenant-Governor of Manitoba, 1882-8.
[8]Mr. and Mrs. Leckie may have been Major and Mrs. Robert Gilmour Leckie, who, like the Brookses, were living at this time in the Eastern Townships.
[9]Unidentified.

165 To Louisa Macdonald

My dear Louisa   *Earnscliffe Sept.* 10, 1887
    I have just returned from Toronto and am going up again on the 13th I shall pay you a visit ere long as I must see about the trial of the election petition filed by Gunn.[10] I think you can scarcely blame Joanna under the circumstances. The chance of visiting the Rocky Mountains & seeing the Pacific was too good to lose. It might never offer again – They will shortly be back. Agnes writes me she is going to bring little Daisy down with her. I dare say Agnes & Hugh will meet somewhere on the journey across the continent.
    Although very hard worked I am in good health and weigh 180 pounds. Hugh's health is not good, and Gertie is a little alarmed about it. His present trip with Brydges will be of service to him. Love to the Professor.

Always affectionately yours
John A. Macdonald

166 To Louisa Macdonald

My dear Louisa   *Earnscliffe Oct.* 14, 1887
    I send you a cheque for fifty dollars which I shall charge against your $1000 in my hands. In the Spring if you want $50 more for your carpet I can give it you. We are all well here. Daisy is at a boarding school and Mary has Maria McP[11] with her. Love to the Professor,

always yours
John A. Macdonald

167 Mary Macdonald to Louisa Macdonald

My dear Auntie Lou   *Earnscliffe Dec.* 10, 1887
    I had a letter from cousin Joan the other day in which she said you were not very well. I hope you will be better by the time this reaches you.

---

[10]Alexander Gunn, his unsuccessful opponent in the general election of 1887.
[11]James P. Macpherson's daughter.

We are all quite well here. Papa is as usual flourishing. I dont think I ever saw him looking better than he is just now. I suppose you know that we have little Daisy with us now. We brought her down with us from Winnipeg and is a weekly boarder at Miss Harmon's school. Some of us go for her every Friday and she goes back Sunday afternoon as she is too young to get up Monday morning to be at school at nine o'clock.[12] She takes great pains with her lessons. Mother received a letter from Miss Harmon the other day in which she praised Daisy both for her good qualities and industry at her lessons. We were out for a drive yesterday which we enjoyed very much. Mother gets up early every morning and goes out to feed her fowls. She has a great many and takes a great pride in them. Mother has gone out with Daisy to bring a lady home to breakfast. How is Dr. Williamson I hope he is better than when I last heard. I am going to coax Papa to take me down to Kingston the next time he goes. I so long to see you all again. The worst of it is that he goes generally for so short a time. But now dear Auntie as it is now nearly half past eleven at which time we have breakfast, I think I must say goodbye with love from Papa and Mama, Maria, Daisy and myself,

I am always your affectionate niece
Mary Macdonald

168 To Louisa Macdonald

My dear Louisa   *Earnscliffe Dec. 10, 1887*
    You must have been highly gratified at the result of the election trial. I intended to have gone up but it was thought more politic for me to be absent unless subpoenaed by the other side. The judgement had all the more effect that I did not appear on the spot to help to get up the case in my favour.
    I should think that the Kingston Grits must feel pretty small.
    I am chained by the leg here just now and cannot leave town for the moment as the negotiations with Washington are going on,[13] & I am receiving cypher messages hourly which require immediate answer. I must therefore postpone my visit until the Christmas holidays.

[12]Miss Harmon's Ladies School was at 49 Daly Avenue, about a mile from Earnscliffe.
[13]A Joint High Commission, meeting in Washington, primarily to discuss the Canadian fisheries.

We are all well here. Little Daisy comes here every Friday night and stays until Monday. She is a very nice child and is rapidly improving at school. Love to the Professor. Always my dear Louisa,

yours most affectionately,
John A. Macdonald

P.S. The $10900 for the water stock was a good price. I added $100 to it and with $11000 made the purchase of Confederation Life Assurance stock.

J.A.MD.

169 TO LOUISA MACDONALD

My dear Louisa   *Earnscliffe Dec. 23, 1887*
     I am sorry to hear from Annie Macpherson that you are not so strong as you should be. Hugh is here just now and in good health. I am so busy that I am obliged to tell my constitutents at Kingston we cannot have a triumphant demonstration just now. Agnes and I and Hugh will however go up on Monday to spend a day at Kingston – *on one condition* that we will live in the car where we can sleep quite comfortably.
     Now *mind*, if you make any attempt to provide beds for us we will turn round & return at once to Ottawa.
     I dare say Christmas bills are coming in so I send you a cheque for 1st January

Allowance	250.00
Interest	35.00
Christmas box	15.00
	$300.00

Love to the Professor.

Affectionately yours
John A. Macdonald

P.S. I have received today the T. & Loan cheque from Annie.

174

My dear Professor   *Ottawa Dec. 28, 1887*
  I send you a cheque for $20 for the McDowall window.[14]
  We got down here very comfortably and found Mary & Daisy well.
With love to Louisa,
                                                        always yours
                                                      John A. Macdonald

My dear Sir John,   *Kingston Dec. 31, 1887*
  Before the year closes I must not omit to thank you for your kind
attention to the matter of the MacDowall window. I have duly received
the cheque and handed it over to Mr Cumberland. I have also received the
books you spoke of.
  Louisa has I think been the better in health for your visit, and goes
up this evening to take tea at Mrs John's. We hope to see you soon again.
  Most heartily wishing yourself and Lady Macdonald, (Lady Macdonald will please excuse the inadvertent inversion of the proper order) a
happy new year, and the same to Mary and her neice, I am always
                                                        Truly yours
                                                      Jas. Williamson

My dear Professor   *Ottawa Mar. 27, 1888*
  I am greatly distressed about Louisa. The account of her health is
most unsatisfactory and I should be greatly alarmed were it not for her
wonderful powers of recuperation. I shall go up for a day, the moment
that I can be spared.
  We are all well here, including Mary, who however has not stood
the winter well.
                                                        Sincerely Yours
                                                      John A. Macdonald

[14]Probably a memorial window to the Reverend Robert James McDowall (1768-
1841), a pioneer Presbyterian minister.

My dear Louisa   *Earnscliffe April 2, 1888*
    I send you the April remittance.
    We are all longing for the advent of Spring and warm weather. I long for it in order that you may get out for a little fresh air. As for myself I am trying to get through our session as soon as possible. So as to run up and pay you a visit. We are all well here.

Affectionately yours
John A. Macdonald

My dear Louisa   *Earnscliffe Apr. 27, 1888*
    Dr Sullivan & I had a talk about you yesterday. He says you are not strong, but on the whole pretty well. He speaks however in the strongest terms of your refusal to keep quiet. Complete rest, he says, is your best medicine, and you wont take it. He objects especially to your going up & down those stairs.
    Now my dear Louisa you really *must* take better care of yourself or you & I will quarrel.
    We are all pretty well here. Agnes suffers much from neuralgia in the face but is otherwise well. I am hurrying up the business of the Parliament as fast as I can and I hope in a few weeks to be able to go to see you.
    Love to the Professor,

affectionately yours
John A. Macdonald

My dear Louisa   *Earnscliffe May 29, 1888*
    On Tuesday last we got through a very successful session during which we didnt meet with a single reverse. On Wednesday Lord Lansdowne left for England & India much to the regret of all who knew him.[15]

[15]Lord Lansdowne, after leaving Canada, became Viceroy of India.

Lady Lansdowne was if possible still more popular— The day they left Ottawa they both came to bid Mary goodbye. Agnes was absent having gone to Dansville to bring her brother down here for a while. To show you the terms Lord L. and I were on I enclose you the parting note he sent me. I am sure the Professor would like to see it. Pray take care of it & return it at once. I shouldnt like to lose it on any account.

Colonel Bernard is awfully broken up but the most patient invalid I ever saw.

Hugh is with us, looking well. As the papers will tell you I am busy in the work of reconstructing the government which keeps me here for a while. You see Sir Charles Tupper has left us to go to England in his old office—[16] Poor White is dead[17] & must be replaced and Mr McLelan[18] the Post Master General is to be Lt. Governor of Nova Scotia and I must find some one to take his place. So soon as I accomplish this I shall pay a visit to you and my other constituents of which I shall give due notice. I have stood the work of the session pretty well and hope soon to get a little rest. Annie writes to Joanna that you are wonderfully well & paid a long visit to her mother. That is as it ought to be. With love to the Professor. Believe me,

yours affectionately
John A. Macdonald

Dont forget to return the letter. You can show it to Maria & Annie.

176 To Louisa Macdonald

My dear Louisa   *Ottawa Sept. 3, 1888*
Yes we are all back again but living in a rented house as Earnscliffe is in the hands of masons & carpenters and will be in that condition for some two months. We had a pleasant tour through Cape Breton but I was tired of our seaside sojourn at Dalhousie altho the hotel was comfortable & the guests pleasant enough.

[16]High Commissioner in London.
[17]The Honourable Thomas White (1830-88), Minister of the Interior, 1885-8, died April 21, 1888.
[18]The Honourable Archibald Woodbury McLelan (1824-90) was Lieutenant-Governor of Nova Scotia until his death.

I will have to run up on the 11th to Kingston but will not consent to your giving up your room.

I think I shall accept Mrs McIntyre's invitation & then I shall be close to you.

Agnes goes up this week to the North West for some weeks and therefore cannot be at Kingston.

Little Daisy goes next week to the convent school near Montreal.[19] It is the best school of its kind in Canada. Mary is as usual but altho' well for her is very fragile.

With love to the Professor, believe me,

affectionately yours
John A. Macdonald

177 TO LOUISA MACDONALD

My dear Louisa   *Ottawa Sept. 28, 1888*
I send you a cheque for $150 being the bal. on your allowance due 1 Oct.

Agnes will be back in Ottawa D. V. on Monday next, which will greatly please Mary & myself.

Always yours
John A. Macdonald

178 HUGH JOHN MACDONALD TO LOUISA MACDONALD

My dear Aunt   *Winnipeg Nov. 10, 1888*
When I wrote to you on Monday last I had no idea that you were ill and you can imagine how shocked I was to receive on Tuesday a telegram from my father saying that he had been called to Kingston by your sudden dangerous illness. I telegraphed him asking him to keep me informed of your progress and to let me know if I should go down. He replied not to come down as you were getting better and today I got a letter from him to the same effect, so I hope soon to hear that you are

[19]The Convent of the Sacred Heart at Sault-au-Recollet.

recovering rapidly. My father has promised kindly to let me know if there is any relapses so I am resting happy in the assurance that in this case no news is good news.

And now, my dear Aunt, I will not worry you with a long letter but will only add that Gertie joins me in much love and also in a fervent prayer that you may soon be restored to your wonted health.

Ever affectionately yours
Hugh J. Macdonald

179 HUGH JOHN MACDONALD TO JAMES WILLIAMSON

My dear Mr Williamson   *Winnipeg Nov. 20, 1888*

On Sunday I received the news of my dear Aunt's death,[20] and although I had been prepared by a letter from Annie I felt that it left a blank in my life that could never be filled and that I had indeed lost a friend. You too will feel the loss greatly for you and she had lived together for so long that I dont think either of you realized how much you were to each other, and I daresay you will even be surprised to find what a change her death will make.

But grieved as we naturally are at this present time we ought not to forget that death must have been a happy release for her, for during the last few years her life was full of suffering and she was able to enjoy but few pleasures. I hope she passed away painlessly and that her last hours were peaceful.

I would have given a great deal to have been with her at the last, but what I heard from the East did not lead me to suppose that the end was so near and I had even begun to hope that her recovery was not impossible.

Goodbye my dear Mr Williamson, and may God bless you.

Affectionately yours
Hugh J. Macdonald

180 HUGH JOHN MACDONALD TO JAMES WILLIAMSON

My dear Mr Williamson   *Winnipeg Jan. 7, 1889*

Many thanks for your kind letter of the 28th Ult. from which I was glad to hear you had passed your Xmas in Ottawa and had eaten your

[20]On November 18.

Xmas dinner at Earnscliffe, for had you remained at home the day would have recalled painful recollections and you would have been oppressed by a feeling of loneliness, though I know Aunt Maria and the girls would have done their best to cheer you up. I am pleased to hear what you say about Mary, and that you think her mind is gaining strength. I formed the same opinion while I was in Ottawa and I feel sure that a great part of her childishness would pass if they would only cease treating her as a child. If you will kindly let me know when Johnnie's schooling is to be paid for, and how much is due I will at once send it to you. I never paid regular remittances, but Aunt Louisa used to write to me when payment was due & I used to send her the amount she required to pay it.

New Year's Day here was as fine as any one could wish, though the want of sleighing considerably lessened the number of callers, and the streets looked very dismal and deserted. I, of course, paid no calls but spent the morning in the office and the afternoon in my smoking room quietly reading Green's "History of the English People".

The weather continues wonderfully mild and open and the citizens of Winnipeg are saving about $40,000^{00} a month in fuel, no small item as you will see. The coal dealers wear gloomy looks but everyone else is cheerful, as well they may be for the weather is charming.

My wife joins me in love to you as well as to Aunt Maria and the girls.

Yours affectionately
Hugh J. Macdonald

181 TO JAMES WILLIAMSON

My dear Professor   *Ottawa Jan. 11, 1889*

We have not heard a word from you since you left us after Xmas.

We can only suppose that you quite threw off your attack while here or you would have let us know it.

I now wish you on the part of Agnes and Mary as well as myself many happy New Years.

We are well here & impatiently waiting for winter. It has at last turned cold and we hope the snow will come by & bye.

We have at last got the carpenters and painters out of the house, which really now looks quite nice. It is the pride of Agnes' heart, and she is never weary of showing it off to her friends. My part of the work in paying the bills will shortly begin.

By the way a large photo of myself came down from you the other day. We didn't want it here so you might as well have kept it, unless indeed you didn't want to give it houseroom.

Today I am 74 years old – a fact which brings serious reflections. I am in fairly good health for my age, but can't expect that to last very long. As my work increases faster than my years, I must soon call a halt.

Do write us now and then and believe me,

sincerely yours
John A. Macdonald

182 TO JAMES WILLIAMSON

My dear Professor   *Ottawa Jan. 19, 1889*
Col Bernard will be very much obliged if you will lend him the book on gout you mention. He will take care of and safely return it. If you will send it to me by book post, I can forward it to Montreal & save postage.

We are all well here and enjoying the first winter's day we have seen.

Yours always
John A. Macdonald

I forgive the Principal[21]

183 MARY MACDONALD TO JAMES WILLIAMSON

Dear Dr Williamson   *Earnscliffe Feb. 18, 1889*
I am going to keep my promise of writing a few lines to you. I hope you are well & taking care of yourself. We had Madame Albani[22] staying here the week before last and Mama gave an at Home for her, at which I was at. I enjoyed it *so* much & was very little tired. She sang for me on my birthday, was it not kind of her? I was charmed with her voice. Etta

[21]What Principal Grant was being forgiven for is not known.
[22]Madame Albani was born Marie Louise Emma Cecile Lajeunesse at Chambly, Quebec. She became one of the great prima donnas of her time.

Macpherson is with us just now & is enjoying herself very much I think but now dear Dr Williamson I think I must close, begging you to excuse this short letter & with love from us all to you, I remain,

yours affectionately
Mary Macdonald

184 HUGH JOHN MACDONALD TO JAMES WILLIAMSON

My dear Mr Williamson   Winnipeg Apr. 18, 1889
    I was very glad to get your last letter and to hear you were well.
    I agree with you in thinking Mr Abbot's speech in the Senate on the foreign trade relations of Canada a very able one, and only regret that it was not delivered in the Commons as the proceedings of the Senate excite little interest and comparatively few people take the trouble of reading the reports of what is said and done there. We intend to leave here for Banff on Monday next and to remain there for three or four weeks for the benefit of little Jack's health. He seems all right again since he has been able to spend most of his time in the open air, but the doctor says he requires change so we are going to try what Banff will do for him. It will be awfully stupid there at this season of the year, but three weeks will soon slip away, and besides his health is of more importance than anything else. Business is picking up a little but money is still awfully scarce and it is next to impossible to get it in. However things promise better this Spring than they have done since the end of 1883 and we all look forward with hope to the present season, so there are few cloudy brows to be seen though empty pockets are plentiful enough.
    While we are at Banff I expect we shall see my mother and her brother Col. Bernard, who intend to spend the summer there, unless he finds the mountain air too strong for him, in which case he will probably push on to the coast.
    A letter from Johannah has this moment arrived telling me you are in Ottawa. I hope you found my father well. This session must have been a trying and fatiguing one.
    With love to all in which Gertie joins, I remain,

affectionately yours
Hugh J. Macdonald

185 To James Williamson

My dear Professor   *Ottawa Apr. 25, 1889*
    I cannot possibly leave Ottawa until after prorogation and it is impossible for me to say when that will take place. We hope to close by Tuesday or Wednesday next but the the opposition by their loquacity and obstruction may keep us still longer. Should it be necessary to make the transfer[23] I must ask you to see to its being made without waiting for me. I shall visit the city as soon as I can.
    We are all well here & send love.

                                                Yours sincerely
                                                John A. Macdonald

186 To James Williamson

My dear Professor   *Ottawa Apr. 29, 1889*
    The business of Parlt drags slowly and wearily on. There is I think no chance of its being prorogued on Wednesday.
    I think therefore you should not wait for me. I greatly regret not being able to join you in the melancholy duty.

                                                Yours affectionately
                                                John A. Macdonald

187 From James Williamson

My dear Sir John,   *Kingston May 12, 1889*
    I was so sensible how much any Member of Parliament, and especially you who have the heaviest burden to bear, must feel himself weary and worn out towards the close of the Session, and how exacting were the duties of your position as Premier, that I forebore to urge you to be present at the transfer. I do not wonder, that it has been as I feared, that you have felt the strain, and that you have been unwell. On the 3d of May George

---

[23]The transfer of the body of Louisa Macdonald to the family plot in Cataraqui Cemetery.

Macdonnell,[24] John McIntyre with Alexander and Richard Macpherson,[25] were present with me in the melancholy duty of witnessing her interment beside her mother as she had desired.

I would fain hope you will soon get rid of departmental work as much as possible. Surely you have enough else to do without it. Come up at all events and see your Kingston friends as soon as you conveniently can. I cannot promise that it will give you much rest, but it will give them great satisfaction, and your rest afterwards will be all the more enjoyed. Catherine has had the house thoroughly cleaned for you, and the best room ready.

I received on Friday a letter from Hugh at Banff with good news of Jack's health which I trust is now fully restored. I suppose Lady Macdonald and Colonel Bernard will also by this time be at the springs or on their way thither. Kindly remember me to them both, and give my best love to Mary from,

yours affectionately
Jas. Williamson

188 To James Williamson

My dear Professor   *Ottawa June 21, 1889*
We hope to leave here in the first week of July for the seaside. Hitherto the weather has been so cool here that there was no necessity for our running away from Ottawa.

Little Daisy will go with us and Maria Macpherson. Mary is going to have Marjorie Stewart with her as a sort of governess or companion.

I won't forget my contribution to St. Andrew's Church. I send you my cheque for $35.60.

Perhaps you might run down to R. du Loup during the summer, & look in upon us. I shall write from there after seeing my people stowed away. With much love from us all.

Yours always
John A. Macdonald

---

[24]George Milnes Macdonnell, Q.C., a Kingston lawyer, brother of the Reverend James Macdonnell of St. Andrew's Church, Toronto.
[25]Two of the sons of Allan Macpherson, oldest son of Colonel Donald Macpherson.

P.S. I shall visit Kingston in September – just as well to let present Anti Jesuit excitement[26] to exhaust itself.

189 MARY MACDONALD TO JAMES WILLIAMSON

Dear Dr. Williamson   *Riviere du Loup July 10, 1889*
     Thank you very much for the nice book you sent me. It was so very kind of you to think of me. I hope to read it soon, and I am sure it will be very interesting.
     This is such a nice place: we have some lovely drives. We have Daisy with us this summer and she is enjoying herself very much. She goes bathing with mother every day and I am going down to watch them all some fine day. I hope you have been keeping well since I saw you. Please give my love to all at Aunt Maria's when you see them, and with much love also to yourself, believe me,

yours afftely
Mary Macdonald

190 TO JAMES WILLIAMSON

My dear Professor   *Riviere du Loup July 30, 1889*
     This is the last day of July or next to it, so to save my credit, I send you a cheque for $100 for St. Andrew's Church. You said something about a tablet but I have mislaid your letter & do not perfectly remember its contents.
     Let me know whether you would prefer the money for a tablet, or on the Church debt. I hope you will soon come down to see us here.

John A. Macdonald

191 HUGH JOHN MACDONALD TO JAMES WILLIAMSON

My dear Mr Williamson   *Winnipeg Aug. 27, 1889*
     Many thanks for your letter of the 19th from which I was glad to learn that you enjoyed your visit to Riviere du Loup and left all well

---

[26]Opposition to the Quebec government's Jesuit Estates Bill, which compensated the Jesuit Order for the loss of its estates in 1800.

there, when you turned your back on the sea and directed your steps homewards. I am particularly pleased to hear that you think so well of Mary. During my long sojourn with my father last year I, of course, saw a good deal of her and I became perfectly convinced that her mind was developing and that she was becoming more of a woman and less of a child than she had heretofore been, though in many respects she was still very childish. This, however, is I think accounted for by the fact that both my father and mother generally treat her as a child and that her companions, when not people well advanced in life, are as a rule much younger than herself. She is a gentle amiable girl and no one who sees much of her, can help being fond of her.

The agitation, if agitation it can be called, about the proposed abolition of the dual languages and the separate schools still goes bravely on both in Manitoba and the North West, and although the Imperial Parliament may prolong their existence, their days are numbered and before long they will both be things of the past. The feeling in the Territories on this question is very strong and I hope the Dominion Government will see their way to offering no opposition to the proposed changes as the vast mass of the settlers in the West are already in favour of annexation and I should be sorry to see anything happen to increase this feeling.[27]

On Sunday evening I heard the Rev. Mr Beakin of Edinburgh preach a really capital sermon and as we had Principal Grant in the morning we were well served on that day at all events. Gertie joins me in love to you all and, I remain,

affectionately yours
Hugh J. Macdonald

192 To James Williamson

My dear Professor   Ottawa Dec. 2, 1889
I shall do my very best to be present on the 18th at the Jubilee of Queen's University.[28] Agnes will accompany me, but we can only be at Kingston for a day. All well here.

Affectionately yours
John A. Macdonald

[27]Hugh was clearly correct about Manitoba sentiment on the issue of separate schools, as the Schools Act of 1890 was to demonstrate. His belief in the possibility of annexation was probably less justified.
[28]Queen's was founded on December 18, 1839, by a small group of Kingstonians meeting in St. Andrew's Church. John A. Macdonald was one of the group.

193 FROM DAISY MACDONALD

My dear Grandpapa,   *Sault-au-Recollet Dec. 8, 1889*
    I am sure you would like to have a letter from your little puss. I hope that dear Grandmamma is better. Cousin Marjorie wrote and told me that Rex sent his love to his little sister. Tell Grandma that her little girl is quite well and sends her love. There is to be a great feast this week. I hope that my little god son is quite well and growing a big boy. Give my love to Mr Pope,[29] ask him to give me his address so that I may write to him. We have a great deal of snow and we play in it every day. Give my love to Mary and all, and much for yourself.

I am, your little puss
Daisy

194 TO JAMES WILLIAMSON

My dear Professor   *Ottawa Dec. 16, 1889*
    Agnes & I propose D.V. leaving here on Tuesday for Kingston. We shall arrive on Wednesday morning and if you don't object will breakfast with you. I am obliged to leave Kingston on Tuesday night for Toronto, where I have a business engagement for Wednesday morning, which must be attended to. All well here & send love.

Yours affectionately
John A. Macdonald

Pope will be with us.

195 FROM GERTRUDE MACDONALD

My dearest Sir John   *Winnipeg Dec. 31, 1890*
    The ring arrived quite safely yesterday & I am delighted with it. It is lovely & just what I have wanted for some time. Thank you & Lady

---

[29]Sir Joseph Pope (1854-1926) was Sir John A. Macdonald's last private secretary, from 1883 to 1891, and later first Under-Secretary of State for External Affairs. He wrote a two-volume biography of Macdonald, *Memoirs of the Rt. Hon. Sir John Macdonald* (Toronto, 1930).

Macdonald so very much, & believe me, I shall always prize it greatly, & take every care of it. I am expecting to hear from my sister all about her Christmas dinner. It was so good of you to ask them & they were so charmed. I hope you had plenty of snow, xmas is so unlike xmas without it. We are having an unusually mild winter. I think our climate must be changing. When is Miriam to be married? I think Mr Harvey used to be in the bank here & is very musical, I did not meet him, but asked him to a dance which he could not come to as he was leaving for the east. I must write & congratulate Miriam.[30] Annie Macpherson wrote Hugh about him when he was leaving Kingston for Winnipeg. I wonder if it is the same man. We are now pretty well settled in our new house & are very comfortable. It is dainty & pretty my friends say, which is good news to me. Jack has just come in & wants to know to whom I am writing & says, "well, give him my love". He is growing such a big boy, & I grieve to say, uses all the *slang* of the day. Good bye dear Sir John. With love to you all & again thanking you for the ring, believe me,

> very affectionately
> Gertrude Macdonald

196 FROM HUGH JOHN MACDONALD

My dear Father   *Winnipeg Jan. 7, 1890*[31]
    As there is no train from here to the East tomorrow, I write today to convey my congratulations and good wishes to you on having reached the 76th anniversary of your birthday. I know that my letter will reach you on the 10th, instead of the 11th as it ought to do, but if I do not write today you will not get my letter until the 12th and I prefer to be a day too early rather than a day too late. I wish you, my dear father, many happy returns of the anniversary of your birthday and I hope you will be long spared in health and strength to govern and direct the fortunes of our young Dominion, for should death or ill health remove you from the helm I see nothing but ruin or chaos before us. If the Grits come into power, they will go in directly or indirectly for annexation, by

[30]Miriam Macpherson married Robert Harvey, who worked in the Bank of British North America in Kingston and was for many years organist and choirmaster of St. George's Church.
[31]Really 1891. Hugh had committed the common January error of writing the old year's date.

which we will be merged in our powerful neighbour and all our aspirations of ever becoming a powerful nation, linked by the strongest bonds of affection to the Mother land, will be at an end. On the other hand, now that Sir Charles has abandoned active politics there is no one ready and able to receive your mantle, when it falls from your shoulders. Sir John Thompson is apparently the only one of your colleagues who is possessed of first rate ability, and he has the reputation of being a Nova Scotian rather than a Canadian which lessens his influence with the Members from the other Provinces and besides the fact of his being not only a Roman Catholic but a pervert[32] will render him unacceptable to the great body of Orangemen, on whose votes we so much depend. John Henry Pope or Tom White[33] might have held the Party together, but at present I see no one capable of doing so. Besides there is practically no Conservative Party in Canada at the present time. There is a very strong "John A" Party, but many of the members of which this is composed acknowledge allegiance to none of your colleagues and I fear a process of rapid disintegration will set in, when any one else attempts to take command.

Gertie was simply charmed with the ring you sent her, which far surpassed her fondest and wildest expectations. It is really awfully handsome and is a Christmas present fit for a Lord. The weather continues very mild and as yet we have nothing you can call sleighing. There is a little snow on the ground and, on those streets paved with cinder blocks, a sleigh slips along easily enough but carriages and wagons are still in use over the greater part of the city. This want of sleighing spoilt the New Year's visiting and the number of callers was very small. I astonished myself by paying 15 visits and have not yet ceased congratulating myself on having come out of my shell in such brilliant style.

Stewart[34] appears very sanguine about Sutherland's[35] chances of carrying through the H.B. Railway and I am sorry to hear that you do not share in his hopes. However nous verrons.[36] Sutherland has not yet returned to Winnipeg and as Mrs S. went down a short time ago to join

[32]He was a convert from Methodism.
[33]Pope was Minister of Agriculture, 1871-3, 1878-85, and Minister of Railways and Canals, 1885-9. He died in 1889. White died in 1888. He had been Minister of the Interior, 1885-8.
[34]Stewart Tupper, Hugh's law partner.
[35]Hugh McKay Sutherland, Winnipeg contractor and lumberman, president of the Hudson's Bay Railway.
[36]The Hudson's Bay Railway was not completed until 1931.

him I dont suppose we shall see him for some time. I suppose Daisy has
gone back to the Convent. With love to my mother and Mary, I remain,

affectionately yours
Hugh J. Macdonald

197 FROM GERTRUDE MACDONALD

My dearest Sir John   *Winnipeg March 7,1891*
A *thousand congratulations* upon your *grand victory* in Kingston,
& all over the country. The Grits are "In the soup" over again & the
country is saved. Kingston has done nobly & has given you the splendid
majority that you ought to have. Winnipeg has also distinguished itself,
& we are all more than proud of Hugh's great success. He is the hero of
the hour here & men & women alike are singing his praises. I am glad
now that he came out as it has done him a world of good. He is in excellent spirits & looks so well & it has shown *him* what he really is thought
of here at least. Hugh's great drawback has always been his extreme
modesty. I am so sorry about Mr Colbys defeat,[37] his daughter seems to
feel it very much. Poor Mr McMicken[38] died early this morning the result
of a severe cold caught ten days ago. He was a dear old man & will be
greatly missed. How glad you must be that the elections are so well over.
You must be completely tired out, & will be glad of a well earned rest.
Hugh has just come in to Luncheon so I must close, he & Jack join me
in much love & believe me,

most affectionately yrs
Gay Macdonald

198 FROM DAISY MACDONALD

My dear Grandpapa,   *Sault au Recollet March 8, 1891.*
I am writing this to congratulate you upon the result of the Elections.
I am so very glad you got in. You could not tell how hard your little puss

[37]The Honourable Charles Carrol Colby, President of the Privy Council, 1889-91, was
defeated in the riding of Stanstead, Quebec, in the election of 1891.
[38]Gilbert McMicken (1813-90) was an old colleague. During the Fenian Raids he
had been Macdonald's chief agent on the frontier. Late in life he entered politics
in Manitoba and was, for a time, Speaker of the Manitoba Assembly.

prayed for you in my thoughts all the time. I hope you will be able to take some rest after these busy anxious days for I am afraid you will be ill. All the girls were so excited as they had some one of their relations interested in the result but we are nearly all conservatives.

With love & kisses to all I remain,

your loving child
Daisy.

199 FROM JAMES WILLIAMSON

My dear Sir John,   *Kingston Mar. 9, 1891*

I cannot forbear troubling you with a few lines now that the heat and smoke of the fight are over, and the victory is won. Not 24 hours had passed from the time you left the house here when the street was illuminated by a huge bonfire in honour of your triumphant return, industriously fed by the Nickles and Lows and a crowd of rejoicing young people, while a deeper though less demonstrative joy gladdened the hearts of thousands of our men and women. The result was indeed a matter for no ordinary thankfulness. It was achieved at a critical time like the success of 1878. Then after years of gloom and depression the people exultingly woke to find themselves free from the incubus of Grit misrule which was crushing the life out of the country, and now by the victory of 1891 we have been happily delivered from threatened and irremediable evils to our prosperity and our very existence. While I give all honour and praise to the wisdom of the policy which carried the Dominion in 1878 I no less admire (——[39] Mr Blake) the wisdom which led you in 1891 to dissolve Parliament and appeal to the country, and has thus enabled you to give an unmistakeable quietus to projects alike of folly and of treason, and to strike chords which will be re-echoed by harmonious notes throughout the whole extent of the Empire.

Your own health has suffered in the sharp struggle with the enemy. Be careful of it if not for your own sake, yet for that of your friends and the Dominion. I trust that the loving and watchful attentions of home, and the return of milder weather will set you all right again. Hugh's triumphant return must have been highly gratifying to you.

[39]Indecipherable.

191

Mr Marshall who writes the editorials in the News is a candidate for the Professorship of English Literature in the R.M.C. I consider him a young man of worth, ability, and culture, as certificates from those who know him well will more fully show. There are I believe a number of candidates in the field, but I feel confident that he would make an efficient Professor. Please keep him in view.[40]

Remember me kindly to Mr Pope. I am still a little shaky as this scrawl will show, but I was out yesterday for the 1st time on my legs again, and walked to Church with thankful heart for all His mercies.

I am with love to Lady Macdonald and Mary,

yours affectionately
Jas. Williamson

200 TO JAMES WILLIAMSON

My dear Professor   Ottawa Mar. 10, 1891

Many thanks for your very kind note.

The Kingston election was indeed a great triumph— I am slowly – very slowly gathering myself together again – I have not been out of the house since I arrived here, but this is a fine day & I shall drive to Council.

I must reciprocate the advice you give me. Take care of yourself. Lady Macdonald & Mary send their love.

Always yours
J.A.MD.

201 HUGH JOHN MACDONALD TO JAMES WILLIAMSON

My dear Mr Williamson   Winnipeg Mar. 16, 1891

I was much distressed to hear from your letter of the 9th Inst. of your fall on the crossing. Fortunately no bones were broken but the shock and jar to the system must have been very great and I do not wonder at your being placed hors de combat for a time. I hope no evil results will

[40]He did not get the job.

follow it and that you will soon be as well as ever again. The majority that my father obtained in Kingston must have astonished friends and foes alike, and was most gratifying in every way. My majority here was equally surprising for Isaac Campbell[41] had the whole place canvassed before I came out, and I had only 9 days to work in, exclusive of Sundays. The Hudson's Bay Railway cry helped me very much, and I attribute my return to a speech which Campbell made against this scheme in the local Legislature a year or two ago. I went into the fight most unwillingly and shall seize the very earliest opportunity that offers to escape from political life and resume the even tenor of my way. I may be obliged to sit for the whole Parliamentary term but nothing will induce me to seek re-election, for a political career is not one in which I would succeed and the life of a politician is distasteful and more than distasteful to me. Since my election I have not been able to do my work as my office from morning till night has been filled with people wanting employment or money and if this sort of thing goes on I don't see how I am going to make my living.

The weather here is cold, clear and enjoyable and everyone is looking happy and bright.

With love to Aunt Maria and the girls, I remain,

affectionately yours
Hugh. J. Macdonald

202 TO JAMES WILLIAMSON

My dear Professor   *Earnscliffe Mar. 31, 1891*

On the whole I think you are right in your determination to remain a Housekeeper. My wife is of the same opinion.

You know I must pay the rent from Louisa's death till 1st May. Please let me know the amount.

Hoping you will long be spared to us. Believe me,

sincerely yours
John A. Macdonald

[41]Isaac Campbell, Q.C., of the Winnipeg firm of Hough and Campbell, represented South Winnipeg in the Manitoba Legislature, 1888-91.

My dear Professor   *Earnscliffe Apr. 6, 1891*
I send you a cheque for $560 which will settle rent to 1 May next. We
are all well here & preparing for the Session.

Yours always
J.A.MD.

204 HUGH JOHN MACDONALD TO JAMES WILLIAMSON

My dear Mr Williamson   *Ottawa May 19, 1891*
    Many thanks for yours of the 8th. I was very sorry to learn from it
that you were so unwell. In this changeable Spring weather you really
ought to take care of yourself for diarrhoea is terribly weakening and,
with the thermometer changing as much as it is doing at present, is very
hard to shake off.

    I am happy to say that my father, who went home from the House
last Tuesday afternoon awfully used up, is now very much better and
I feel sure a week's rest would put him on his feet again, but I know there
is not the slightest chance of his being induced to take it. Last week he
kept away from the House it is true, but he went to the Council every
day and worked at Earnscliffe with Joe Pope. Indeed I think he would
have been in his place in the House as usual, had not the Governor-
General, who was very much alarmed about him, called at Earnscliffe on
Wednesday morning and insisted on his absenting himself. The truth is
that the Cabinet is so deplorably weak that there is no one to take his
place. He would not care to hand it over to a French man, as they already
have the important Departments of Militia and Public Works and with
the exception of Sir John Thompson, Foster[42] & Charlie Tupper[43] there is
not an English speaking Member of the Cabinet worth his salt. I wish
the session was well over and my father away at the sea. Unless some-

---

[42]Sir George Eulas Foster (1847-1931), Minister of Marine and Fisheries, 1885-8,
Minister of Finance, 1888-96, Minister of Trade and Commerce, 1911-21.
[43](Sir) Charles Hibbert Tupper (1855-1927), Sir Charles Tupper's second son. At
this time he was Minister of Marine and Fisheries.

thing unforseen happens I intend to run up to Kingston on Saturday, spend Sunday and Monday with you and get back on Tuesday, that is to say if my doing so will not put you out.

Yours affectionately
Hugh J. Macdonald

205 HUGH JOHN MACDONALD TO JAMES WILLIAMSON

My dear Mr Williamson   *Ottawa June 2, 1891*
    You disappeared so suddenly yesterday that I did not know you had gone and spent some time looking for you in the house and through the grounds before I realized you had actually taken your departure.

My father had rather a bad day yesterday but rallied through the night and today is decidedly better, that is to say stronger. There is, however, no other change in his condition and I have no hope of his recovery. I am happy to say he is free from pain and his expression is as peaceful and happy as it has been since his seizure.

I asked Joe Pope, who attends to the telegraphing to keep you advised as to his condition, so what I am now writing will be stale news when it reaches you.

With love to Aunt Maria and the girls, I remain,

affectionately yours
Hugh J. Macdonald

Index

Draper, William Henry, 81; ministry of, 51n.
Drinkwater, Charles, 104
Dufferin, Marquess of, *see* Blackwood, Frederick Temple
"Dungeness", 9, 43, 44, 45, 49

"Earnscliffe", 23, 132, 140n., 150, 162, 170, 177, 180, 194
East Greenwich, Connecticut, 9
Edgar, Sir James, 124 and n.
Edinburgh, 14; High School, 14; University, 14
Elections, general: (1874) 113; (1878) 130n.; (1882) 132; (1891) 190-2
Elliot, Gilbert John, Viscount Melgund, 156-7
Ewart, John S., 148

Farmers Protective Union of Manitoba, 153
Farrer, Edward, 148
Fenian Order, 16; raids, 16, 102n., 190n.
Fish Creek, battle of, 156n.
Fisheries, negotiations with the United States, 173n.
Folger, Henry, 129
Folger Brothers, 129n.
Fort Garry, Man., 17
Fortnightly Review, 141, 150
Foster, Sir George Eulas, 194
Fredericton, N.B., 165

Galt, Sir Alexander Tilloch, 98, 99n., 101n., 102, 103, 104, 131
Galt, John, 101n.
Galt, John, Jr., 101
Gardyne, Catherine (Macpherson), 29 and n., 82 and n.
Gardyne, David Bruce, 29
Gardyne, Thomas M.B., 82 and n.
Geological Survey of Canada, 77n., 124 and n.
Glenora, Prince Edward County, Ont., 13
Goulburn, Henry, 30
Gowan, Sir James Robert, 85, 133, 157
Gowan Scholarship, 158

Graham, Sir James, 30
Grand Trunk Railway, 81n.
Grant, George Munro, 151, 158, 181, 186
Grant, Sir James Alexander, 107, 110n., 113, 138, 144
Grant, John, 136, 137
Grant, Mary, 137
Grant, Penelope, 137
Grants, provincial, 106 and n.
"Great Coalition", 85
Great Eastern, 104
Great Western Railway, 140n.
Greene, Charles Collins, 50
Greene, John, 5
Greene, John Ward, 4-5; death of, 5
Greene, Margaret (Clark), 4-5, 8-10, 11, 27, 52, 71, 137; death of, 10; letters from, 28, 97-8; letters to, 31-50, 52-71
Greene, Nathanael, 50
Greene, General Nathanael, 4, 5, 8
Greenway, Thomas, 149
Gunn, Alexander, 146n., 172

Halifax, N.S., 165
Hall, Dr. C. B., 116
Hall, Elizabeth, 20, 91n.
Hall, George B., 20; death of, 91 and n.
Hargrave, Man., 168
Harmon, Miss, Ladies' School, 173
Harper, Francis Archibald, 13, 29, 30, 47, 58, 62, 69
Harper, Wilhelmina (Macpherson), 13n., 51, 52
Harvey, Robert, 188 and n.
Hay Bay, Ont., 13
"Hazeldell", 13-14, 93n.
Head, Sir Edmund, 73, 81, 92
"Heathfield", 13-14, 95, 96n., 101, 102, 108, 114, 116, 120 and n., 126
Henderson, James A., 123
Herbert, Henry Howard Molyneux, 4th Earl of Carnarvon, 102, 104, 139
Heron Bay, Ont., 164-5, 167
Highclere Castle, 139
Hough and Campbell, 193n.
Houghton, Col. Charles Frederick, 153, 156

199

74, 76, 79; letters from, 31, 54-5
—— James Shaw, 12; death of, 13
—— Jean (King), 17-18, 144; death of, 145
—— Sir John Alexander; appointments, as Imperial Privy Councillor, 139, as Prime Minister, 104, as Queen's Counsel, 48, as Receiver General, 48n.; birth of, 2; date of birth, 2n.; death of, 3; illness of, 58, 79, 97, 99, 110-11, 130, 131, 138, 144-5, 194-5; Kingston property of, 100; law practice, 131-2; law studies, 3; letters from, 28, 34-54, 56-83, 89-97, 98-105, 106-10, 111-13, 115-16, 117-20, 120-2, 124-5, 125-7, 130, 135, 138-42, 143-4, 146-7, 149-50, 151-2, 154-5, 156, 157-8, 166, 172, 173-5, 175-8, 180-1, 183, 184, 185-6, 187, 192, 193-4; letters to, 28, 97-8, 105-6, 114-15, 117, 120, 122-4, 125, 128-9, 134-5, 135-7, 146, 148-9, 149-50, 151, 152-4, 155, 156-7, 158, 166-7, 168-9, 175, 183, 187, 188-92; marriage, 103; offer to, of Solicitor-Generalship, 48; political career, 3, 26, 112; rumour of peerage for, 171; speculation in land, 25-6, 131; travels, 27, to England, 28-31, 80, 139, 142-3, 158, 163
—— John Alexander (son of Sir John A. Macdonald), 52n., 53, 55, 56, 57, 58; birth of, 51; death of, 59n.
—— John Alexander (grandson of Sir John A. Macdonald), 18, 132, 163, 180, 188, 190; illness of, 182, 184
—— Louisa, 12, 13-14, 20, 27, 31, 36, 53, 72n., 76, 77, 79, 82, 83, 89, 92, 95, 111, 118, 119, 121, 129, 131, 132, 143, 151, 152, 156, 167, 180, 183n.; death of, 179; illness of, 122, 147, 149, 154-5, 175, 178-9; letters from, 127, 128, 134-5, 135-7, 144-5; letters to, 72-4, 79-80, 92-4, 95-6, 98-105, 107-8, 109, 113, 116, 118-19, 120-1, 125-7, 130, 135, 138-42, 143, 144, 146-7, 149-50, 157, 163-6, 169-74, 176-9; sale of land, 126
—— Margaret, see Williamson, Margaret
—— Margaret Mary Theodora, 20, 22-

3, 112, 113, 115, 116, 118, 121, 123, 124, 126, 127, 129, 138, 140, 141, 143, 149, 154, 155, 157, 162, 163, 165, 168, 169, 172, 175, 177, 180, 184, 186, 187, 190, 192; birth of, 110 and n.; illness of, 132, 135, 137; letters from, 125, 158, 168-9, 172-3, 181-2, 185; letter to, 111
—— Mary Isabella "Daisy", 18, 20, 132, 144-5, 148, 154, 163, 172-3, 175, 178, 184, 185, 190; letters from, 187, 190-1
—— Susan Agnes (Bernard), 20-3, 103, 105, 107, 109, 111, 112, 114, 115, 116, 118, 119, 121, 123, 124, 125, 126, 134, 137, 138, 139, 141, 142, 143, 144-5, 150, 155, 157, 158, 162, 168, 172, 173, 174, 175, 176-7, 178, 180, 184, 186, 187-8, 192; created Baroness Macdonald, 23; letters from, 163-6, 167, 169-71; trip to British Columbia (1886), 163-6, 177
—— William, 12
Macdonald, John Sandfield, 109; Ontario ministry of, 106n.
Macdonald, Tupper, MacArthur, and Dexter, 18
Macdonald, William K., 97
Macdonnell, Archibald John, 86, 92, 93, 94, 98; death of, 99n.
Macdonnell, Daniel James, 128, 184n.
Macdonnell, George Milnes, 183-4
Macdonnell, John Alexander, 87, 102n.
McDowall, Robert James, 175n.
McGee, Thomas D'Arcy, 108
McGuire, Thomas, 123, 128
McHugh, Hugh, 101
McIntyre, John, 123, 127, 184
Mackenzie, Alexander, 143; ministry of, 112, 113, 124, 125
Mackenzie, George, 93n.
Mackenzie, Sarah, 93, 96
McKerras, John Hugh, 140
Mclean, Allan Neil, 95
Mclean, John, 95n.
McLelan, Archibald Woodbury, 177
Maclennan, James, 115, 151
Macleod, James Farquharson, 154
McMicken, Gilbert, death of, 190

Williamson, Margaret (Macdonald), 12, 13-14, 18, 27, 31, 36, 49, 50, 51, 53, 66, 73, 74, 76, 77, 80, 82, 83, 89, 90, 94, 96, 98, 99, 102, 103, 105, 108, 109; death of, 119; illness of, 70, 116, 118; letters from, 33-4, 79, 110-11; letters to, 71-2, 89, 91-2, 94-5, 96-7, 111, 112; marriage, 72 and n.
Wilmington, North Carolina, 40, 42
Wilson, Ann (Macpherson), 28n., 66, 70
Wilson, James, 141, 142
Wilson, Thomas, 28, 31

Windsor Castle, 29
Winnipeg, Man., 164, 167, 168, 170, 173
Winnipeg *Free Press*, 148
Winnipeg *Times*, 148 and n.
Wise, Henry Ellison, 156
Wistar Association, 38
Wolseley expedition, to Red River, 17, 111n.
Wood, Edmund Burke, 109

Young, John, Baron Lisgar, 139n.